A Child Called Whore

Denise Wilson

Turtle Publishing
www.turtlepubs.com

All rights reserved

Copyright ©2012 by Denise Wilson

Library of Congress Catalog Card Number

ISBN 978-0-9852361-1-3

Printed in the United States of America

Dedication

I dedicate this book to my two favorites in this world.

My husband, who has taken the time to know me, and then made the commitment to love all that he knows about me.

My personal God who has never stopped creating light out of some of the darkest moments imaginable.

Dear Mother

One word, then two, then three
Repeated over and to the end

Always there, always waiting
To hinder the years that mend.

18 years after the Beginning

Dear Mother,

I finished unpacking my bags today and found all of your tapes inside. Isn't it funny how all those tapes take up no space at all in my suitcase but almost all the space in my head?

They will get regular play here on this competitive campus in Cambridge, Massachusetts. They will play during tests and in the middle of oral presentations, through dates and breakups, and alongside decision and indecision. They will be here through it all, carrying your words, your tone, and your anger over and over and over again. The dark memories will flood in, keeping the words company, and my potential at bay.

Sometimes, I will survive the tapes, almost unscathed. Other times, college will be too hard or the culture too lonely or the lost love too wrenching. Then, I will curl into a tiny ball and the darkness will crowd in around me, lapping greedily at all that remains light and hopeful inside of me. I will sob. I will scream. I will beg to be delivered from the pain inside. In the tiniest of balls, the tightest of fetal positions, I won't be sure to survive until tomorrow.

But, for now, I am one step out of the door now. I am a freshman in college, 3000 miles away and one stride forward along this convoluted pathway toward healing. I have no idea what lies ahead. I don't care really. All I know is that what lies ahead will be better than what lies behind.

I hope that my leaving gives you the freedom you wanted. You will be able to date now, to find a man to love you and care for you. None of that was possible before, when I was there with you. I hope that now you have the elusive ticket to your happiness in hand... the one that you were quick to remind me remained outside your reach while I was there with you.

If I made you so miserable, may I ask just one question?

Why did you cry when I left?

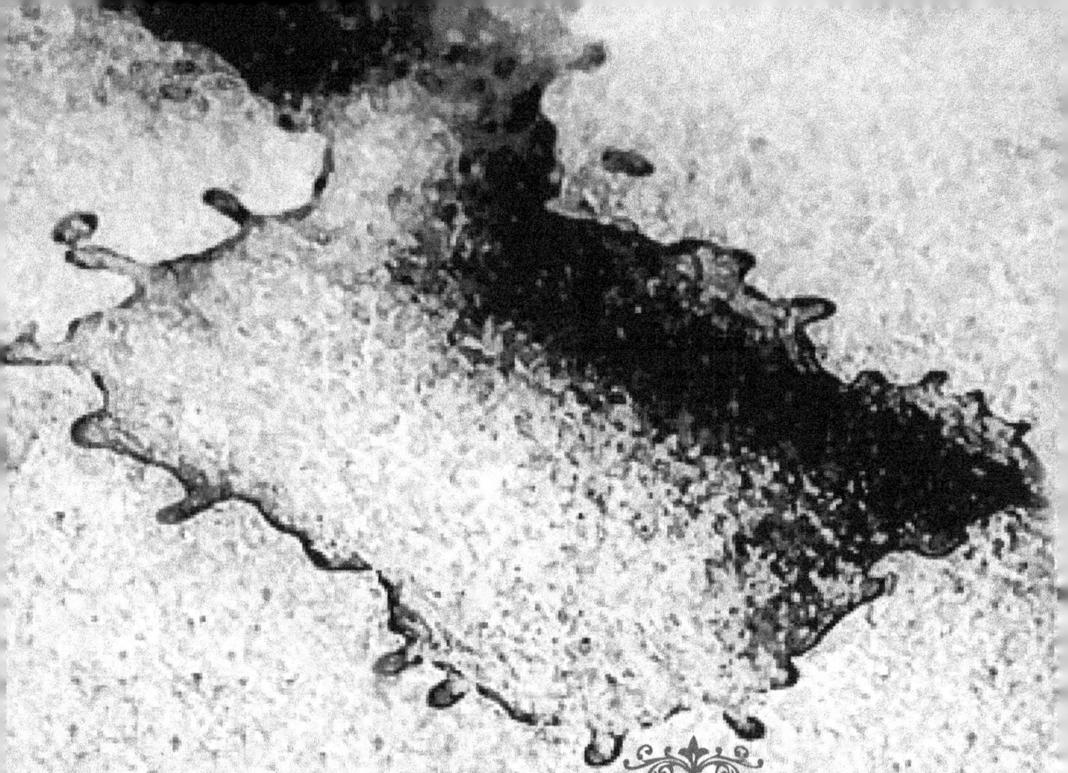

Stained

one day, i became a slut
long before my first kiss
a day after, i turned into a whore
even without having sex

The carpet in my bedroom is a 70's myriad of colors with a proper 80's style haircut. A mix of brown, yellow, orange, white, and other scattered colors in between make for a celebration of shag that came shortly after the kaleidoscope of greens that plagued the 60's. Unlike carpets that were true to the style of the 70's, however, all the threads in this carpet have been cut short, absent of shag, and denied the influence of the decade before. Despite its cultural identity crisis, my carpet has the decided advantage of hiding stains quite well. This quality is especially handy to me right now, considering the clumsiness that is a natural part of my adolescence that is at odds with the physical discipline doled out for even the slightest of errors by the woman I call Mother. She is a 100% German woman who quickly escorted me into this world some 14 years ago, much to her ongoing lament and seeming regret.

I am sitting now, on my forgiving, albeit tacky and somewhat stained carpet, with my back toward the stereo, books piled high on my left, open bedroom door on my right, and the twin frame of my childhood bed holding its spot under the open window on the far side of the room. The stereo behind me is an inheritance from my departed sister, who was kicked out of the house at 16. It is a behemoth of oversized electronics that came to be long before Moore's law of shrinking electronics made the stereo an elegant and unobtrusive addition to a room. I can easily reach the large knobs and buttons of my music monster from where I sit to match my many moods. The books on my left are stacked high in several piles, a combination of library and school books, the only interruption to what is otherwise a neat and sterile room. The bed under the window is the softest piece in the room, covered in a checkered yellow bedspread, made in a fleeting moment of love by my grandmother. The bed holds a cornucopia of memories.

Its narrow, twin size has seen many pillows drenched with tears, sheets agitated by nights of horrible loneliness, and a mattress bearing the weight of fear aroused by the intrusion of many multi-legged bedmates. The bedroom door on my right stands wide open, not by my preference, but because any other orientation might provide some privacy that is simply not allowed here.

In other parts of the world, the spring brings lightness and cool. Gentle breezes might be flowing into the room, softening the edges about it. But here, in the Florida spring, the air in my room is still and hot, disturbed not even by a hint of wind, despite the closeness of the ocean, only a few blocks away. In the absence of air conditioning, both at school and at home, I have grown accustomed to the misery often brought on by the heat, the humid, and the still. Wiping the sweat from my brow is as natural to me as it is for a northerner to stomp her boots in the doorway before going into the house.

At first glance, I am just a simple freshman in an average high school in a state marked by one of the worst secondary school systems in America. Born poor, I am counting on the gray matter between my ears and the acute stubbornness that on a good day might be called dogged persistence to get me out of here. On my stained carpet, I am sitting, focused on the latest of my school assignments. Tonight, it is a biology assignment from a teacher who insists on the proper name of Dr. to keep his elite status clear to all of us lowly freshman. My teacher with the doctorate in some field that I do not know, refuses all excuses for incomplete work (including the various delays incurred by chronic childhood abuse). His teaching philosophy includes an insect collection that if not completed to his satisfaction, will keep me in 9th grade forever. I simply must finish the insect collection; it is part of the price I must pay to move beyond where I am today.

On this evening, even with steel walls securely fastened around my emotions, the process of pinning insects to cork board still pierces the tenderness of my young heart. So much for a career as a surgeon.

My persistence outweighs my nagging feeling of distaste and I continue to attach my hard-won and inelegantly trapped multi-legged creatures to the board, via not the most efficient of means. Each creature is centered neatly above carefully written labels describing classification and genre. As I work, I migrate to the most comfortable position for my work, legs spread out before me, one length of slender flesh and bone stretched out on either side of the insect display under construction.

It is in this position that I look up, breaking my concentration to see Mother standing in the doorway. Her body language advertises some latest wave of anger with me. Befuddled, I quickly search my mind and memory for what I could have possibly done wrong. Panicked now, I search through the memories, trying to deflect the rage that is now marching my way. I cannot find any obvious violation of The Rules, however slight. Confused, I am unprepared. Her first words are familiar ones, heard many times before the verbal lashing starts.

"What do you think you're doing?"

To which, I answer the obvious "Working on my insect collection for ..." To which I am, as usual, interrupted:

> "Don't you have any sense? What is wrong with you? What are you ... some kind of whore? Good girls don't sit like that ... do you have any idea what the boys are going to say about you? ...."

Mother continues on in her tirade, somehow convinced, beyond all reason, that I am a 14-year old whore living under her very own roof. She is tragically distressed by the evidence of my cheap behavior. My choice of sitting position so clearly advertises some promiscuity that I am neither guilty of nor even knowledgeable about. Mother is overwhelmed by self-pity because she believes herself to be the victim, the innocent parent who has been saddled with such a worthless excuse for a daughter living in her house.

By the time she is done, my concentration and opportunity to finish the insect collection are gone. Somewhere while hearing myself called a whore for the fifth time and listening to a verbal attack that goes on for 15 minutes or more, I start the internal dialogue in my head, the one that keeps me from falling into the rabbit hole.

> "Boys ... really? Well that would make perfect sense if there were any boys within sight to draw these kinds of conclusions. But it looks like the customer base for my hidden prostitution ring is rather thin this evening, so I thought instead I would entertain myself by working on something as mundane as an insect collection, while practicing positions appropriate to my true occupation which you have so smartly uncovered here today,"

Even with my unspoken sarcasm used as a defense against the attack, Mother's words continued to fly like arrows in the room, sinking deep into the soft spots of my budding sexuality with a vengeance that even time may not heal.

Sticks and stones may break my bones ... but words will only destroy me.

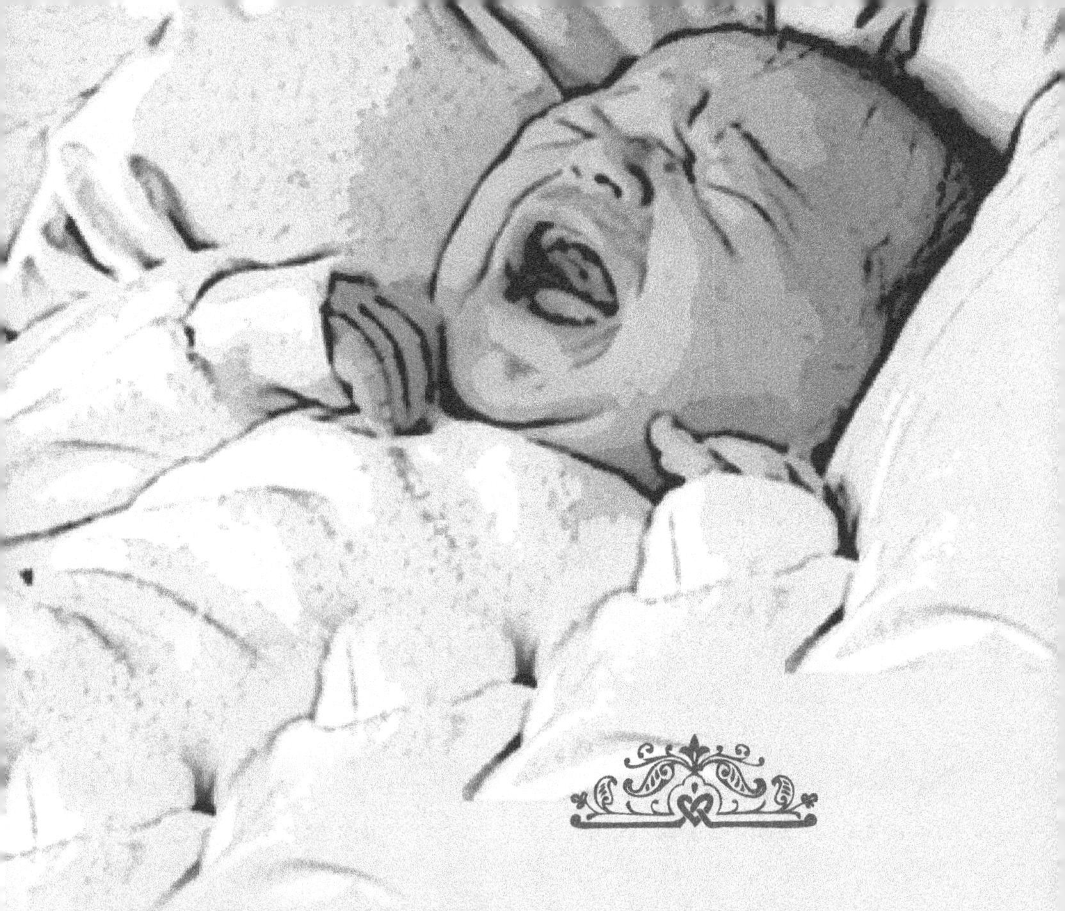

The Beginning

a quiet child
a crazy place
fear runs wild
on Mother's face

I have no memories of my first day of life on this earth, yet like many others, I hear words and sentences and ideas along the path of life about that first day. I create a story in my mind of what it was... a story about Mother's labor and our first meeting.

Among the falling leaves of Autumn, the best friend dashes to the hospital with her young pregnant passenger. Barely into the hospital, in fact still in the waiting room, the second daughter of the family arrives. I weigh in at less than 6 pounds. I am not nearly as difficult as my older sister Mary. Mary had taken a ride on the Prenatal Roller Coaster and had stalled in upside down position, causing a long painful breach labor that Mother would never forget.

Since the difficult business of delivering Mary, Mother had become pregnant a second time. That baby was lost, through a tubal pregnancy. After the operation, the doctors reluctantly informed Mother that it wasn't possible to carry a baby again in her damaged womb.

Did that diagnosis make me a miracle, an unfortunate accident, or a disaster?

Even after the short, relatively easy labor, Mother is still anxious ... scared and prefueled with frustration in preparation for another year of incessant crying. That was the song that Mary had brought with her into this world. And it was what Mother now expected.

Daddy came to the hospital well after I arrived. He was busy, but he came. He held me. He cooed. He tried to love me.

At home, I was a quiet baby. Mother, Daddy, Mary and I lived in a cramped apartment in downtown Chicago, on the corner between one Polish neighborhood and the next. Daddy is Polish; Mother is German. They are not married. Daddy's mother does not approve. Mother's mother does not care. I rarely cry.

One day, it starts to hurt more and more. My tummy first whispers, then whines, then wails. There is not enough. I can no longer sleep. I whimper. I cry. I scream. For days, then weeks. Nothing changes. I hurt. The starvation closes in.

Mother is tired now of the crying. She is ashamed of her own milk. She doesn't want anyone to know. But, now she must tell someone. Her baby is dying. She goes to the doctor. I have the bottle. The wail inside of me ebbs to a whine, then a whisper … then silence. My tummy is full.

My body starts to grow.

I am a quiet baby again. For now.

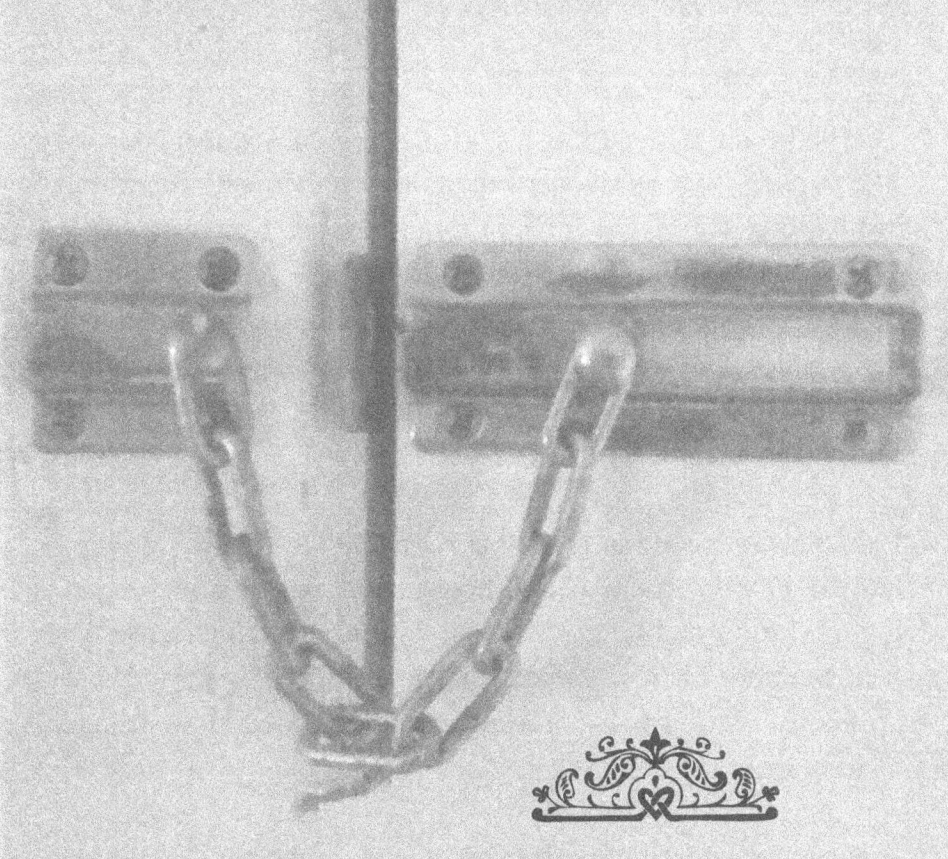

Locked

trapped, panicked, alone
in this cozy room
silly girl
calm down
and sleep right now

The bedroom is small, no more than 150 square feet, but cozy. The twin bed sits on the far wall, its foot underneath the window, overlooking the neighbor's house, not twenty feet from the sill. The other window lies to the left of the head of the bed, overlooking the street from atop a small hill. In summer, the hill looks benevolent to all but Mother who mows it. In the winter, it becomes a precarious mixture of ice and snow that impede child, Mother, and auto alike.

I am playing quietly in the living room, late in the day. I only go into the cozy bedroom when I have to and then, quickly, to grab a toy or clothes or book. Mary is playing outside with the older kids. I am not invited. I play, inside and alone. Soon Mother will be home. The sun has already started to head down the sky, inviting night to come.

It is several hours before the sun will go away, but I am already scared. I play harder, trying to stack buttons and blocks into a magical castle palace that my solitary barbie doll will enjoy. When Mother comes home, I try not to look up. I am afraid. I want the time to stop and daytime to stay forever.

Now, it is all business. Clean up. Wash hands. Sit down. Eat everything. Brush teeth. Go to Bed. It is still early. I am not tired. The fear makes me even less tired. I try to stall, try to make the time last with the eating and the brushing. Mother is not patient. I finish.

I am in my room. I watch the door close. I hear the latch slide into place Locked.

I will be here now for more than 12 hours. Someone has invited the monsters again. They start to leer from the corners, underneath the bed, and inside the closet. They are still small and quiet. But they will grow ever larger, when night comes.

I think about fire. If it were to come, I would have no choice but to break the windows. In my mind, I would then become a child of superhuman strength, hurling a bedpost through the window to exit the house for safety. Or, also in my confident fantasy world, the impossibly painted shut window locks would spring free under the blistering heat of the fire. I would then use that superchild strength to hoist them open and leap out into the fresh night air. Of course. In my mind, I had the evacuation plan all thought out.

I try to close my eyes, to stay in bed, as Mother said. I am not tired. I am still afraid. Sleep will not come. I slide quietly off the bed. Sometimes, I will talk to Mary through the heater vent between our two rooms. Sometimes, I will take out my toys and play. Sometimes, I will try to read, alone ... my only choice. I will try to make myself tired. I will try to not be scared. I will try and try and try.

Sometimes, Mother will hear the noise behind my door and yell. Sometimes, she will unlock the lock and come in, hitting me to keep me quiet and in bed. I will try hard not to disobey.

I have to go to the bathroom. I can't. I don't want to face Mother. I will hold it. I can't anymore. I knock on the door. No one hears me. I knock more. I pound. Mother comes. She yells. I run to the bathroom. I am done. I run back. Now, I am here again. Locked.

I close my eyes. I open them. The monsters come out, all at once. In terror, I scream inside my pillow. Mother hears. She yells. I cry silently. I thrash.

Finally, on a tear soaked pillow and on sheets scrambled by my thrashing, I sleep, exhausted.

The monsters stand by.
In case I wake up, they will be ready.

Hammered

Knock, knock
Who's There?
Fever, Ache, and Pain

Knock, Knock
Who's not There?
Logic, Reason, and Tame

I am six years old. I have more childhood diseases under my belt now than reasons for living. And, today, another one is approaching from the west, like a storm designed just for me and the very few other unvaccinated children in the modern world. It is a Tuesday afternoon, when I first hear the little man riding in on the edge of the storm front, laughing in the corners of my small world, taunting and waving his hammer at me.

By the early evening, the little man pounds on the inside of my skull with relentless glee. I try to count the dots on the ceiling to escape. I have counted them now, three or four times, even in the dim light. They are making patterns and dances of lighter times, creating dreams before me in the darkness.

The little man runs around my head, beating with his hammer at a different part of my fever-stricken head every second. My bed sits near a window that on a better day, or in a home where immunizations are allowed, would be open, breezes fluttering against the slim line of the open curtains. Instead, the breezes stay outside, the windows shut, curtains drawn; the light that makes me smile is locked away, kept out there, while I am in here... alone, hurting, tired.

I could open the windows, but the sunshine lurking outside would only be halfway into the room before the little man would take out his largest of all hammers and beat it against the inside of my skull twice as fast... playing a hard rock tune alongside my feverish skin that could only lead me to scream at him. He is only just the mischievous messenger of a childhood disease that had been extinguished for most kids many years ago. As for me, Mother will tell you that she has protected me from the stupidity of immunization. Something about these long torturous days in darkened rooms with my immune system at war with every single cell in my body is apprently good for me. So good for me that even aspirin would ruin the experience, much less an advanced medicine like Tylenol.   So I suffer. I am alone, crazy hot, and without medicine.

I am still in bed. There is still some daylight lapping around the edges of the curtain, trying to creep in. There are no other noises in the house to smooth the sharp edges of my lonely heart. To my left, on the dark oak nightstand, lay the pills that don't quite take away the pain, despite their homeopathic promise to do so. There are no toys or books or TV. According to orders, I must keep myself quiet and deeply submerged under the covers, to drive the fever hotter and hotter. Then it will break and the little man will vanish, taking his over-active hammer with him.

My cheeks are swollen to twice their size. I can't eat solid food that will make it past the mumps on both sides of my throat. My body fights. Invisible to me, my heart weakens as the fever stays, hot and flushed... another childhood disease underway ... another vaccination that could have been but wasn't.

I close my eyes now, searching for a place where the pain is bearable. Turning one way in my mind, I see the lurking loneliness... another way, I see the fear of another beating, and yet another, I see the shame of being an unwanted child... another girl, an impossible baby, as poor a surprise as there could be.

To place after place, I turn in my young mind. I run through my head ducking ghosts and demons and pain and shame. I am screaming now... as these dark places now tumble down on top of me. There is no place without pain to turn. My eyes frantically search in the nooks and crannies of the dark hour. I am suffocating under the wait. I can't breathe. I no longer scream.

My eyes pop open wide from my dream. The fever has broken. Perspiration fans out across my face. The flush begins to fade. I begin to breathe normally again.

My hope creeps back into my world, wrapped up in the impeccable innocence of childhood. It will stay, until the little man rides in again, wielding his hammer in glee on the wave of another childhood disease that surely I could have done without.

Separated

One last fight
left Daddy behind

A new start
Another different house

I am seven years old. Little Adult has come knocking on the door to my identity; she has been called early in my life to attend to the badness of this place. She had all her tools with her, ready to craft wily ways along my path that would let me make it to the other side. She had her chance to use them on the day that Mother and Daddy had their last fight.

Mother and Daddy both work during the week. Mother is gone during normal banking hours. Daddy works a late shift. When Mary and I are not in school, we wake up alone in the house, while waiting for Daddy to wake up from his night shift. On these days, there is time to play. Daddy will wake up late in the morning. I will be delighted. He will take me into his arms. He will give me the biggest of all bear hugs. He is not all that good at making meals, mowing the lawn, or anything like that. But he is the very best at loving us in the moment, when Mother is not here.

On the weekends, I am used to watching Mother do the chores on the Saturdays, while Daddy is off in the city with grandma doing her chores. I stay home with Mother on these days, rather than joining Daddy. On Saturday, it is quiet and Mother will even once in a while take me out on one of her errands and give me a nibble of attention.

Sunday morning is as idyllic as I can know. We watch StarTrek (yes, the original) in the morning; the house is quiet and filled with the smell of fresh waffles. Mother is content in the kitchen while she cooks the waffles and the four of us sit down to eat breakfast together. It is almost normal.

What happens next is out of place next to the sweet normal morning. Mother and Daddy will now sit on the lawn chairs in the backyard drinking a beer and sharing time together as couples do. My sister and I will play on the swing set. As the first beer turns into the second beer, the fighting will start. The voices will rise as the second beer turns into the third and so on. Full scale drama will now play out in our little suburban scene. We are no longer playing on the swing set as if we are normal. As the beers march on, Mother and Daddy will go inside so that the neighbors don't hear the shouting.

Most Sundays, they will fight until we go to bed. In the morning on Monday, they will go back to their routine. But this Sunday evening, it is clear to Little Adult that something is different. Some piece of heart, exchanged between the two of them and hopelessly battered... can no longer be retrieved and it is time for Mother to go. Mother begins by packing the laundry basket full of essentials. She stops then to resume the fighting. Little Adult picks up with the packing where Mother left off. I know that this fight has now gone from simply angry to dangerous. It is really time to go. I know that there has been too much arguing and pain between parents, too much for kids, too much to overcome. I am hoping that we can leave before something worse than what already is happens. I am tired of the tension, the anger, the noise. I am also afraid. The anger is still expanding. It is rising, filling the house, and overflowing.

As it gets dark, the fighting continues on and on. Mother announces again that we are leaving and begins packing our things. Little Adult takes over again to put everything in its place, all the important childhood things tucked away in a small bag. I don't understand why Mother and Daddy can't just love each other. I am puzzled why Daddy prefers his own mother over his own children, much less the mother that bore them. I have no answers.

I have stopped listening to the fight, confused by the lack of anything useful in it all. Little Adult sits me down on the couch. We are finished with the packing. I burrow into the cushions now. I am scared, small, and alone.

Peeking up, the fighting is growing worse again. Mother sends us across the street, down the hill, to the neighbor's house. A young blonde girl named Gwen lives there. In her house, the air is warm; there is no conflict here. We play. We laugh. We relax.

Back there, up on the hill where our small house sits, Daddy is too angry. He uses his hands. It gets worse. Mother is picking us up now, packing us into the car. We are driving away. I don't say goodbye to Gwen. I don't know yet that I'll never be back here again. We are driving away. Little Adult is quiet.

There is no way to manage this ache. The loss is too much. Sometime very later on, sleep will come. But for now, the silent stream of tears falls like a spring rain, drop after drop onto an invisible face over a blank child.

Beaten

Spare the rod
Spoil the child

abuse the rod
destroy the child

No way to tell really which is the worst ... the day before, the day of, the day after. They each have their own rhythm of fear, pain, and loss. They each take a little bit more away from what is needed to survive.

The day before. Despite what Mother says, I am a pretty good kid. I am tempted to do little wrong and from that little temptation, I choose even less to do wrong because I am so afraid of Mother. But Mary is not that way. She seems to search out trouble and has the talent for finding it. I will choose today between Mary and Mother. Mary doesn't like it when I don't go along with one of her plans and she is much bigger than me, even more than what our 4 years difference in age would explain. When I don't go along with Mary, she is quick to show her anger. She will beat on me for a long while and even after, she will still want me to go along with her.

On the day before the beating, I am quick to cave in. I give up easily and go along with Mary. Mother will usually find out. More often than not, she will ask me about what we did. Less often, I will tell her the truth. Something about the truth makes me stronger, even though in the moment it will hurt so much I will be tempted to start lying forever forward. I have that sinking feeling in my stomach now, dread mixed with fear, as Mother is getting angrier and angrier. She is yelling now, telling me all about how bad I am. She is telling me what I deserve. She is telling me that it will happen tomorrow as soon as she gets home from work. It is a clever idea for Mother to wait a day before she uses the belt. It gives the fear inside of me a real chance to explode into full blown anxiety and send my self-worth into free fall.

On the day of the beating, while Mother is at work, I always hope as children do that Mother will choose not to. Yet she always chooses to go through with her threat. She never forgets the bad yet has no trouble forgetting the good. The belt and beating are routine. She first makes sure that we both know why we deserve it. She will ask the questions until we give the right answer. Truth be dammed. She makes certain that we know how angry she is. She wants us to know how we have disrespected her. It is all about her. The child is irrelevant.

She does my sister first. I listen to Mary scream. I hide further and further into the corner as far away as I can get from Mary on the other end of the house. When my sister rushes past me, I want to die. It is my turn to get what I deserve. One strap, Two strap, Buckle me too ...

Sometimes, I scream. Sometimes my heart shatters. Sometimes both. I run. I cry. I sleep. I wake up the next day. My eyes are swollen. My face is puffy. The bruises are here. Mostly black. Some blue. They hurt.

The day after is the worst. Mother likes to dress me on these days. She will insist on giving me a bath. When she reaches the bruises on my white skin with the washcloth, she will make me look at them. She will ask why they are there. She will ask me if I deserve them. I am afraid. I will agree and agree again. Yes, I deserve them.

She will pull my panties up quickly, my pants up harshly so the bruises will smart under the fabric. She will send me on my way after I agree once, twice, three times that I deserve this.

When it is over on the outside and the bruises fade from black and blue to purple to yellow and then to nothing, the bruises inside will still be there. They stay long after the ones on the outside heal. They will continue to remind me.

I deserve to be beaten. I deserve the anger. I deserve to cry. I deserve all that I have.

Deserted

I am just a floating ship
Sailing on God's lonely sea
Submarines of despair
Passing silently beneath me

It is spring. The night is calm and the heater quiet. I lie in my narrow twin bed content. I fell asleep many hours ago and now I enter into a dream of fantasy and flight. I am flying through the air on a trapeze, a skilled and respected part of a nameless, ephemeral circus. The air is light around me. There is no weight to my body nor to my burdens. I am in the air again now, falling after a grand flip from one trapeze bar to the next. As I reach the net below, my toes barely touch before the lightness of spirit propels me upward again, back to the trapeze, back to floating with not a care in the world. I am swinging back and forth now, gaining speed and preparing for the next trick as the audience watches and waits.

The mood changes now. The audience is angry. My feet are growing heavier, then my body. I am falling now, faster than gravity will allow. I will hit the floor soon. The anger is waiting for me. Terror creeps in around the edges of my lightened spirit. Still falling, someone is shaking me.

I open my eyes. Mother is here, by the side of my bed. Angry. I panic, scrambling to think of what I have done wrong this time.

"Where is she?"

Who? What? I think. I am still fuzzy from sleep. A smile leftover from the good part of the dream still floats around the corners of my mouth. Think. Think. I must answer, before Mother gets angrier. The smile is making her angrier. She thinks I know something. She thinks I am lying. I must stop the residue of a smile that remains on my face. I pull the corners of my mouth down. I am confused. I am just a little girl waking up from a fanciful dream. I am confused as to why fancy does not come with me to the waking world.

As the fog of sleep rolls out the door, I grow to understand from Mother's angry words that Mary is gone. She has crept out into the night. She has run away from home. Mother thinks I know where Mary went. She demands that I tell. I don't know. I am afraid.

We don't find Mary that night. By the next day, she is with Daddy, gone for good. After crawling out the window the night before, she hid in a tractor parked in the construction zone near to the house. She stayed there while Mother searched and then she waited for Daddy to come get her. Daddy came in the night. He took Mary with him. He left me behind.

Mary, Mother, Daddy... they are the only three I have in the world and they have deserted me. The morning after Mary left, the amazing lonely years started. Long days, weeks, and months of staying inside the house alone. I will be so often sad, lonely, and desperate for people, anyone to talk to, to play with, and even to hug me.

I love school. I love it because there are people there and things to do. The other kids don't like to talk to me. I am too strange. But, they are there. And, I am not alone. The teachers talk to me. They help me. Sometimes they smile at me. Then the darkness goes away, for just a moment.

Summers are the worst. Long weeks of no school, no kids, no one but me and the demons to play with. I am alone in the house for at least eight hours every day. I am alone until Mother comes home from work. She will fix me a quick dinner. I will have ten minutes, maybe twenty of her time. Then the men will come over. They will drink beer with her. She will read cards for them, tell them their futures. They will talk for hours and laugh. I will be invisible.

Sometimes one of the men will put me to bed. Cliff and Larry are two of my favorites. They will laugh and look me in the eye. They will see a person. Cliff has some pity in his eyes. Larry tries to hide his. They know about the loneliness. They try to give me a few minutes away from it. They do what they can. I do not know that I am lucky. They just smile, tuck me in, and leave. Nothing else happens. They do not touch me, except for a gentle hug. They are kind and honest men. But they want Mother, not me.

After I am officially in bed, I lie in bed, wide awake listening to them. They will get louder as the beers get emptier. I listen to them talk and laugh. I will cry myself to sleep. The pain will rise, reach the top, and then break. Often, I will fall asleep in the middle of a sob, depleted. On the good nights, I will plan the next day one half hour at a time, carefully filling all the time with something that will keep the loneliness at bay.

The next day, I will follow my plan. Little Adult knows the limits of my brain chemistry. She will allow me an hour or two of TV at a time. If I watch more, the fog will roll into my head making the thoughts go haywire and pushing me off an ever near emotional cliff into an ugly and black pit of loneliness. In the morning, I am allowed to watch an hour or two of game shows. My mind works to solve the puzzles. The loneliness is held back. In the afternoon, another TV window is allowed so that I can watch a sitcom or two. In between TV times, I will play with dolls, read my books, and play with my favorite toy. The toy is red.

I try to stay with the plan. But I fail and fail again on many many days. No matter how meticulous Little Adult plans my schedule, I fall off the wagon. In the middle of the TV runs in the morning, I will start to cry. I will curl up into a little ball on the living room floor, screaming for someone to save me from the loneliness. Sobbing. Begging. Please, please, please... over and over again. Wishing to be magically swept up and moved to a place where there are family and people. Some days, I will not be able to stop and I will call Daddy and beg him to help me. Pleading. He will not come. Why? I don't know. I don't understand.

No one ever comes. Not a single time. Not a Daddy, not a friend, not a one comes to the door. No one will hold me through the tears. The good days are those only with tears. On the bad ones, I am screaming and pounding against the wall, the door, the floor.

Terror.

Desperate.

Alone.

Tempted

Turning
I faced evil

Tempted
I reached out

Ashamed
I turned away

There comes a point for everyone where we have to choose right or the wrong will overtake us. At the turning point, we can't choose to just sit still anymore. Choosing right suddenly becomes something we must do or we will be be chased down by the wrong and thrown into the darkness until we are dark ourselves. Before I turned ten, the darkness was a passive soul, sometimes just sitting over there in the corner, sometimes taking moments to smother me, sometimes delighting in my tears. But it was never a true part of me.

At the age of ten, it started to creep up from the inside. I was tempted to give in and to use it to control, to have power, to take charge of what I could. Tempted. To start walking down the road that would repeat the cycle. The darkness called. I listened. I took its hand and I walked with it.

It was spring and Mother was in a good mood. We were on Saturday errands and when we happened to walk past the pet shop, I pleaded to take a look inside. Mother indulged me. We walked in and I found the two cutest hamsters in the place. They were two females that once in my hands, I called Flopsy and Mopsy. Mother helped me set them up in their plastic cage. We laughed together. I felt Almost Normal. I would take better care of them than Mother of me. I assumed I would.

Four weeks after Flopsy and Mopsy moved into my little bedroom, a gaggle of hairless babies showed up in the cage, bald, pink, and ugly. So much for the two females theory. Mopsy appeared to be the boy in the crowd and within a day, had killed and eaten many of the babies. I cry. I move him to a separate cage. The babies escape from the cage. Mopsy escapes. Flopsy is all that is left.

Flopsy is not a happy hamster. She seems frustrated, clawing night after night at her plastic cage, seeking any or all escape. Scratch, dig, scratch she goes in the middle of the night. I am trying to sleep, to get away from Mother's latest words. I want to run away into a dream, have a few hours away from the pain. Flopsy has other ideas. Scratch, dig, scratch.

Mother tells me to shut her up. I pick her up from her cage and drop her on the floor. She is quiet. Very quiet. Ten minutes. Then scratch, dig, scratch.

I am another person now, somewhere else. I don't say to myself that I am hurting her but I must know that I am. I am not stupid. I am a bad girl. I drop her over and over again. I want her to be quiet. I want Mother's words to stop. I want it to be quiet. I want and want. I am tempted. I am only wanting for me. I don't care about her, the little furball who has done nothing at all to deserve hurt.

I hurt her anyway. She bites me. Makes me more angry. I am stronger and have more power. I hurt her again. Her internal bleeding is now obvious. It is the middle of the night. Now, I am scared. I know what I have done. She no longer moves. I have killed her.

For a moment, I feel a sick rush of feeling good. I have power. I can control. With this dark anger, I can be in charge. I am tempted. I want to keep the control.

For a moment in time, I am perched on the choice. I am tempted to take the hand of darkness and walk. I am wanting control. I am tired of having none.

Who knows why I let go, turn the corner, and walk the other way. If I was raised in the church, I might call it God. But all I know of God is the name that gets thrown around in anger and the one who never listens when I cry for Him.

Oh but He just did. Listen that is. I don't know and I can't see but He took my hand, gently and led me out of the darkness.

I took shame and guilt with me from that dark place and held them close to me. I dragged them around for weeks and weeks that quickly turned into months and months.

But one morning, the sun streamed in the small window in my corner bedroom. It reached out and shamelessly snatched the shame and guilt from my soul where I held it close and dark.

It said,

"Mine .... your shame and guilt are Mine.

In return, I give you Grace."

I had no names for these things, but I knew what they were.

Groomed

I was a girl
Later a woman

But now
I am in between
struggling to be seen

Small wins make you try for more. Therein lies the problem.

At the end of freshman year, I begged and pleaded to Mother ... let me shave my legs ... Please ... let me be just a little bit like the other girls. A little bit less of an outcast.

Mother gave in, kind of. I was allowed to shave up to the knees, no more. And only using cream; No razors allowed. Sure. Fine. The upper half, along my thighs was covered in blonde hair anyway. Someone needed to be up close to see it. And no way I was letting a boy get that close.

Anyhow, there I was one day in the bathroom, ever so merrily shaving my legs. I looked at my hands and saw my fingernails, cut as short as could be. I had long fingers with sturdy rounded fingernails. Wouldn't they look just so feminine if I could grow a fraction of an inch of white nail beyond the living bed? Ah yes. I was a teenager. I easily convinced myself that I had to be able to let my nails grow or all hopes of a social life would collapse underneath me. Over a set of ten fingernails, no less.

Stupid idea, it was. Mother called me in to have my fingernails cut to the quick again. She had been drinking. I was in a mood. Bad combination. I said no. She said "Come here .... NOW". I said no. I am sitting on the floor. She throws the clipper at me. She says "NOW" again. I say no. She is saying more things now. They hurt. I am tired of giving in, of feeling ashamed. I fight back. Stupid idea, it is.

She is kicking me now, in the ribs and stomach. I am in a ball on the floor, not thinking anymore. I only want it to stop. The uncle is over there in the other room. He watches. He looks away. He does nothing.

She kicks a few more times and stops. I don't remember how it ended. I want to know why. Why do Mothers kick their daughters over fingernails? Why? Why? Why? Over and over in my head it goes, until the tears start to bleed the pain away. Why? Why? Why? I am still on the floor. I don't want to get up. I want to know Why. Why so much anger?

Sob once more, then twice, then over again. The Why grows quieter. Sob again.... and quieter still. Then sleep... sweet, dreamless. Healing.

The next morning. We start all over again.

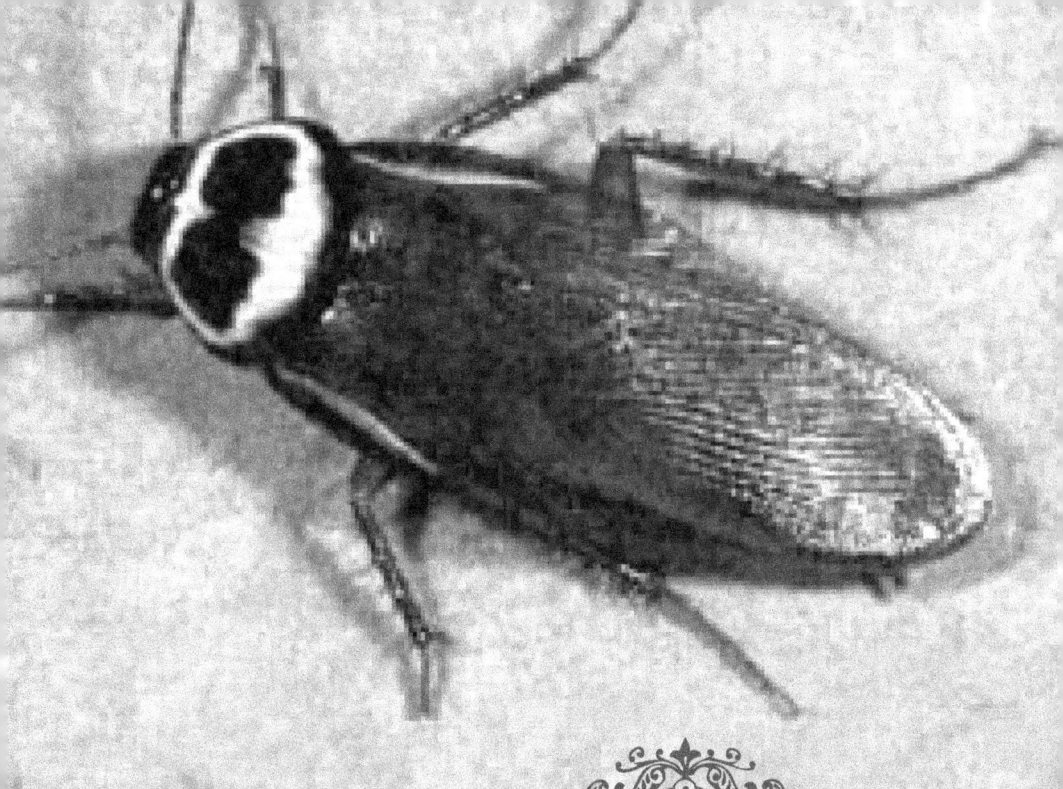

Bugged

Two wings that fly
Six legs that crawl
A feathery light, slinky touch
Across bare skin
Comes to call

It is summertime in Florida. There is no air conditioning. Mother doesn't like air conditioning. The air hangs, hot and muggy around me. The sweat returns only milliseconds after I shower. I dash out of the house, hop on my bike and seek refuge at the library. It is cool and quiet here. The books are some of my best friends. They take me traveling all day long.

But now, the library is closing. I walk out into the twilight. The oppressive heat has relented by almost five whole degrees. Less than a mile of travel leaves my bike and I joined together in sweat. I eat the hot dinner Mother has in front of me. I must. The sweat continues to pour down my face. I am done.

There is one fan in the house. It is in Mother's room. My room has no fan. I am not important.

All of the windows are wide open. The screens are worn with age, holes mixed with rips and ragged edges. There is no breeze in the night. I get up almost every hour to refresh the cold wash cloths wrapped around my wrists. It doesn't matter how late it is before I finally fall asleep, I'll wake in the morning, wet and sticky, merged with the bed sheets. I will roll out of bed in eager anticipation of the shower that will leave me cool and dry, if only for a little while. Really, the heat is hard, but it doesn't make me cry at night. It is a managed problem.

The palmetto bug is a territorial critter; it prefers to hang out near home, which is the nearest palmetto plant. There is a palmetto tree just outside my bedroom window. I know when the slightest of breezes is coming because I will hear it rustling through the large stiff fronds of this tree.

It doesn't take a rocket scientist to figure out that those large oversized flying cockroaches would sneak into Mother's house through my bedroom window. It took a less naive mind than mine though to imagine what they would do next once they were in the house. I assumed that they would politely crawl around my bed into the kitchen to eat the crumbs and politely leave the same way they entered. A nice idea, one that matched my still optimistic view of the world. But, a very WRONG idea.

It is one of those many hot muggy nights that punctuated the Florida summer like cherry blooms in the spring in Washington D.C. I am sound asleep, becoming one with my wet, sticky sheets, delightfully unaware of the twisted mess I am making. I awake with a start. One of those critters is crawling across my arm. I am repulsed, a sick feeling quickly spreading across my stomach, threatening the bedclothes with the remnants of my dinner. I throw the damn thing across the room. I turn the light on. My eyes are bug-eye-wide open. I close the windows. I am scared. Mother is here now. Yelling. "How can you be so stupid? It's hot. Open those damn windows now." Stupid, indeed.

I leave the light on. Mother is here again. Yelling. "Turn that light off and go to sleep, you ungrateful little brat!"

I'll sleep in the bathroom. Mother will find me there. She will yell. Anything but listen.

The bugs are still here, now, night after night. Sometimes I am lucky because they only crawl over an arm or a leg. Sometimes they move onto my chest, sometimes on my face. Still other sometimes, I wake up with one crawling in my mouth and then another crawling around my underwear. No amount of washing takes away the memory of those legs moving across me. No toothpaste takes away the texture of the legs and the fluttering of the antennas. No shower is long enough to erase the feather touch of wings against my most private parts.

No level of tired makes it OK to go to sleep. I try to stay awake, watching for them. I fall asleep anyway. I wake up... to the legs crawling where they may.

Sometime months later, the bugs reach Mother's room. Now there is a criss. The house is treated. The bugs are gone. But the memories are pesticide-resistant.

Erased

Here today
Gone tomorrow

When will it be my turn?

Black cats and white cats and calicos too. Red dogs and white dogs and black ones too. They all came. They all went. Erased as if they were never here at all. They never mattered.

Just like me.

Fiver was a little calico kitten with the characteristic five toes that made him a true calico. Like all the rest, he wasn't allowed inside. A litter box might smell. There might be fur on the carpet. So he couldn't come inside. He was happy outside. He slept in the garage. He played most of the day long. Unlike when we lived in Illinois, he wouldn't freeze to death in the oncoming winter. He would have a few fleas. Mother might discard him for that. But I wouldn't find him a block down the road frozen to the surface of an icy pond. Those days were gone. I didn't have to turn a corner and worry about finding their dead bodies anymore.

Many times during the long lonely summer, I played with Fiver. I knew not to get attached. I did anyway.

I went to a girlfriend's house that day. It was hot, terribly hot and her air conditioning and I were almost better friends than she and I were. We had a cool afternoon. I came home. Mother wasn't home. She had gone out.

I looked for Fiver. I called his name. He usually came to my call and then played hide and seek around the big oak tree. I called him again and again. I tried not to be scared. I went inside and acted as if I only needed to wait and he would come around the corner once again.

I passed the time by cleaning up the kitchen. I took out the garbage, opened the outdoor can, threw the bag over the top... and saw the corpse. The crushed body inside the clear plastic ziploc bag. I was silent. There was no scream inside my shock. Nor even in my pain. I could make no noise at all.

But I could run. I ran and ran and ran until I was at the girlfriend's house again. Her mother was home now. She didn't understand. She told me to go home.

I walked back onto the street. The ghosts walked with me. The little black cat, terribly thin and long dead, under the spring snow in the back yard. Her brother, a tough oversized gray tom, frozen stiff onto the ice. More cats after that. More stories. More tears.

Then Muffin, the little white ball of canine fluff and love whose back was broken by one of the 'mentally disturbed boys' on the school campus where we lived in Illinois. And then, in Florida, Muffin junior was another little white ball of fluff and love who was allowed to stay, tied up to the back tree, until he had too many fleas. Then, he too was discarded. There were many more dogs... Maggie, Skipper, Cindy. Their ghosts grew in number as they all walked alongside of me, their faces haunted. All those many faces were wrapped in a kaleidoscope of Fiver's own fresh corpse, thrown hastily into a plastic bag after he was run over by a car by a driver who was too hurried to check under the wheels.

All the while, I cried. I didn't go back to the place where Mother lived. I walked and I cried. When I was too tired, after the sun was gone, I curled up on a manicured soft green lawn and cried some more. Under the stars and the trees on the lush grass, finally, I slept.

A year later, I turn 17.

This time, the pet daughter left.

Dismissed

Girls like me
Can't

Boys like him
Can

School is a safe place. There are right answers there. And rarely ugly words. Sometimes the people there are extra nice to me. Sometimes they give me awards.

Sometimes their awards come with a dinner, where the people who give the awards want to be seen doing exactly that... giving an award to a bright young adult with a promising future ahead of him.

I don't exactly fit that mold, but they invite me to their dinners anyway. Sometimes Mother will take me to the dinners where they give the award away and where they look good for giving it away. I don't look like what they expected ... with my mismatched, awkward clothes, my stringy hair, my downcast gaze. But, they are too embarrassed to change their minds and give the award to someone else.

The food at the dinners is usually good. There is plenty to drink. Good for me. Not so good for Mother. Many of the dinners, Mother will drink quite a few. As soon as I can, I will slip out to avoid any chance to watch the ensuing dance among alcohol, Mother, and the many men that flocked around her.

On one of these nights, I step out into the parking lot to gaze at the full moon. It is quiet, warm, and peaceful. I close my eyes and let the world be OK for a moment.

I hear the voice in my ear and want it to go away.

"You're Ellen's daughter, aren't you?"

... I still hope she would go away ....

"Yeah"

... she is still there ...

"Well, what a nice award you've gotten tonight. My son, you know him?"

... and my unenthusiastic

"Yeah"

which she ignores, continuing on

"He won the ... " blah, blah, blah...

She goes on for quite some time about the awards her son had won, how wonderful he is and of course, how wonderful his parents must also be. I continue to watch the moon, trying to ignore the speech that marches on next to my ear. Then:

"He is going to be a doctor someday."

which brought on a sigh from me and then my response:

"Oh Really?"

and finally, her punchline:

"Yes, he is going to be the top of his class. You're in his class, aren't you?"

I sense trouble now in her voice, in the way she looks down rather than across at my eyes. This mother went on again for another while to tell me how kids like her son went on to be successful, to graduate at the top of their class, to go to college. All the while, it was a true shame that girls like me could win a few awards here and there, but those awards really would never take me anywhere.

The poor white trash speech ... went on and on and on and on. Girls like me really had no chance. Apparently, I was to watch her son speak at graduation, and then watch him go to college. At the same time, I would return to my proper circumstance, stuck in poverty and shame by some unseen force that she presumed would keep her orderly view of the world right on track.

I am still too young and still too soft-hearted to call this woman a bitch, but my jaw did drop open as she went on and on into the night. Her words started to sound the same after awhile. They were all condescending and unkind. Mercifully, she finally tired of her speech and left (wishing me all the best as she did). The best ... really?

I am getting a little tired of all the Ugly Words, the endless string of put-downs from Mother. Because of Mother, this mother's words were not having their desired effect. Instead of crawling into a hole and accepting defeat as my birthright, I just got angry.

Angry. And Stubborn.

We'll see about your predictions, lady. I ain't read nothin' in the darn constitution that says I ain't goin' at least as far as your son goes. You just wait and see. Really.

Raped

No, I said
to his hands
No, I said
into the silence

No, I screamed
... and was crushed.

September in the year that is Mother's 46th birthday. It is a warm, sunny day. Mother is drinking. As soon as I can, I will sneak out of the house. I will be deliberately vague about where I am going.

I am on my bike. Pedaling slowly. Going to visit my godfather. He is such an oasis in this emotional wasteland of being an adolescent. I am hungry for hugs. Starved for love. Seeking to be heard. All these things, he gives. I keep pedaling.

I am also aware, dimly, that maybe some of his touches aren't quite right. Perhaps he shouldn't be touching me the way he does. I push the thoughts away. I believe in the goodness of people. I believe he will stop soon, because he knows it is not right. He will win this struggle with himself. He must be seeking help. I keep pedaling.

I really have no other choices for those who would care for me. Surely he knows he must stop touching. He is an adult. I trust him. I keep pedaling.

By the afternoon, I will not trust him anymore.

As I pedal home, afterward, the hurting goes inside to the deepest place in my soul and all the parts of my body. I am shocked but the welcome numbness is already ceding to the shame beginning to flood in around the edges.

At home now, Mother calls me a whore and a slut. She says I deserve this, because it is who I am.

The details of the day will always stay vivid. The deepest blue of the sky, the innocent fluffy whiteness of the clouds, the warm comforting heat gifted by an autumn sun. The little duplex that is being painted by my godfather for the next tenant, the uncovered mattress, the feel of the wetness of my legs, the ringing of the word No, as I say it over and over again.

Over and over again. I stopped crying No when he finally broke into me, because some part inside of me also broke, and rattled as the pieces fell away. There was no point in saying anything. He got what he wanted and there was little room for my words or feelings anymore. I cleaned myself up in the shower because I didn't want that feeling between my legs one more second than it needed to be there. I rode home. All the cleaning and scrubbing in the shower didn't help. The feeling was still there, under my skin, inside of me, burrowing… escalating shame.

I wondered for a moment if this is what all godfathers did to take care of their children. I wondered where God was in any of it. I wondered if there was a God.

I walked to the ocean that evening, after Mother was done yelling. My body hurt. My heart cringed.

I crawled out to the very end of a broken down, condemned pier and sat, propping my knees up against a decrepit piling and stared out at the oncoming sunset over the sound that separated me from the Gulf of Mexico.

No one could reach me now, across this vast and empty abyss that stood between me and the world. No one could reach me in this corner of darkness, where I curled into the smallest of balls. No one except

One.

Dear Mother

But if we hope
for what is still unseen by us,
we wait for it
with patience and composure

Romans 8:25

18 years after the Beginning

Dear Mother,

That was just a few of the tapes I just sorted. There are quite a few more, but I'm tired now. I'll leave the rest to collect dust before they suddenly grow a life of their own again.

Right underneath the tapes, in the bottom of the last box at the end of the packing, I found my toolbox. Wow, am I glad it made it to college with me! Tapes and no tools. That would be a disaster and a half... a recipe for quickly dropping out of college. I am soooo not flunking out of this place even though 'intimidated' only begins to describe how I am feeling around all this prestige and smarts up here in Cambridge, Massachusetts.

Here we go. I've pulled out one of the tools. It's labelled Swimming. What can I do with that one here? The river that lies one hundred steps beyond my front door is not only polluted but nasty cold. But they say that there's a big swimming pool on campus, with lots of lanes to swim in even for amateurs like me. It's not the Gulf of Mexico, that's for sure, but it will do.

And then, here is my tool called Planning. That will come in handy in the never ending battle to keep my head above elite academic water and the workload. And, here's Traveling ... that will come in handy on those long plane rides between here and there, where you still are.

When I unpacked the tools, I started to forget about those tapes. I started thinking and hoping. It is possible for me to make it through this undergraduate thing. We'll be all right here. We'll muddle through. We will figure it out.

I hope you're doing well Mother. No sense in harboring ill will. I've got my Tools and you can have your Tapes.

Although, I suppose I'll always wish things would have been different.

Tools of the Mind

Do not forsake wisdom, and she will protect you; love her, and she will watch over you.

Proverbs 4:6-7

School

I am five years old. Today is my first day in school. They call it Kindergarten. I am the kid. Where is the garden? I can barely say it right, much less spell it.

I am afraid of leaving home. I like my little corner on the couch on the far end of the living room. It is 7 little girl steps away from my bedroom. It is a place in the world where I can disappear, where if I curl into a tiny ball, it is almost safe.

The world outside of my little corner is not safe. Mother has made sure of that. I am not angry or sad about this, just scared.

Mother drives me to school today; she almost loves me. I want to be brave. We have walked through the front door now. I see now, all the things around me that are not familiar. Chairs, tables, colors, toys … and the teachers. They are adults. They are not safe.

I start to cry, run to Mother as if this time she will hold me, love me, reassure me. For a moment, her arms are there and holding me. Then they are gone. The tears start to come, building with a life of their own as if to fill their own ocean. A trickle turns to a stream, then to a river, then to a flood. The sobs keep going, shaking my thin little frame as if they will break it. Mother begins to laugh, then leaves. She will go to work now.

I am alone. The sobs still come. The teacher tells me to wipe them away. "Go to class" she says. "It will be all right." I look at her. I want to ask. "All right? What does that look like? How will I know it when I see it?"

I turn now, away from the door where Mother just was, and I walk into the classroom. I am still sobbing but quietly now. The other kids are looking at me. The sobbing quiets more. My eyes are still puffy and red but my mind peeks out of the pain to see. There are bright colors around, letters and pictures and posters. Many, many things to learn.

The teacher is smiling gently. Her eyes look warm, almost safe. My sobs quiet even more, then stop altogether. I listen to the teacher. And my mind starts to learn.

Day after day, school becomes the best and the safest place to be. The eyes of the teacher stay warm. Her words stay safe. I am not scared here, in this classroom place. I sit and listen, hungry to learn. The alphabet, the numbers, the reading ... especially, the reading. I am too shy to read out loud but in private, my eyes will swallow up the words, learning one, then the next. The sentences, one after the other, will cascade through me like a crisp clean waterfall. I am both hungry and excited, lapping up the written word like a starved puppy.

Here in the mind, everything is calm. The learning is safe. I love it. There is hope here.

Travel

It is a snow-covered brutally cold day in rural Illinois... at 8 years old, I am still 6 months away from moving to a much warmer place, far south. For now, I still don't really know that Florida exists ... a place where I will no longer be trapped in the house for days on end during the winter.

It is Monday and Mother is at work. She will work until the evening, well after dark. Then, not long after she comes home, several men will arrive at the door, one at a time. Some will be colleagues, some will be married, some will be interested. I am too young to understand what they do in pursuit of Mother. But I am not too young to understand that I will be lonely this day, the next, and the three after, a pattern that ends only on Friday when the weekend comes. During the five days of the work week, I will have a half hour of time with Mother and perhaps another five minutes from one of the men at bedtime.

I was hopeful. It had been a very successful weekend. The right mix of pleading and doing exactly as I was told had landed me a visit to the library, leaving me with a new stash that now lay neatly stacked in the corner of my small bedroom on the southwest corner of the house. On Monday morning, made cold not only by the conservative thermostat temperature but also by the unwavering acres of snow covered land outside the window, I gladly crawled back into bed after fetching my breakfast... but not before I had pulled a jewel from the stash. I stared at the cover for quite a while, read the plot line on the back and after minutes of savoring the permission to go on this adventure, I opened my book and began my travels. Other days, I might embark on a more predictable and lighthearted adventure with Nancy Drew, suitable for my age. Instead, today, I began a classic tale. The librarian had told me this one was well beyond my years. I ignored her.

As I turned the pages, the characters started to evolve and the language of the master writer created a fabric of circumstance, of struggle, and of richness that the basic language proper to my age level could never do. As more and more pages turned, I gradually disappeared from that small bed and from the cold wintry day. I grabbed my passport and landed in another country far away. I hopped the train and joined these main characters in their living room, warming my cold hands by their roaring fire.

The pages turned, now unnoticed as I grew to know these people in this fictional but masterfully created place. Only my eyes would betray me as eventually they grew tired and ended my whirlwind tour. The end would be temporary though, and I would return to finish this delightful journey as soon as I could.

Courtesy of my local library, traveling had become one of my very favorite pastimes. The places I could go, the people I would meet, and the things I can learn were often nothing like this place where I lived at all. Today, I was traveling in another century, another country, and another culture entirely. The adventure fills my mind completely. Tomorrow, we might take it much easier. Travel closer to home then.

Mark Twain stared at me from the stash on the other side of the room... and agreed with my choice.

Calm

The textbook was neatly laid out on the small desk tucked away in the corner of the sunroom. A cheap white notebook sat next to it; two pencils, sharpened and ready to use, sat at the perfect angle across its lined white pages. The little chair, while it had no cushion to help tolerate hours of sitting, had an old-fashioned, gently sculpted wood back about it that only added to the calm aesthetics of this orchestrated little workplace.

Before beginning, I eased back into the kitchen to grab a small snack, risking an exchange with Mother that would only steal my motivation to return here to the little workplace. Luckily, today, no such encounter came to pass and I slid back into the sunroom, silent and unnoticed.

I paused before sitting, gathering my energy to walk through the gate from this crazy place to a far calmer one. I pulled the chair away from the desk, sat, and tucked both myself and chair close in, merging with the little workplace.

I picked up one of the orange pencils in my right hand, retrieved a snack in my left, and closed my eyes for a moment. Alone in the world inside my head, I looked around to see the chaos dominating the space... ugly words and relentless ridicule clustering around almost every thought I could have. Somewhere though, among fear, anxiety, wound and pain, I saw a little doorway hidden deep in my mind. I found the courage to walk through the littered mess of my own thoughts, and then dashed through the door.

Now opening my eyes, my mind inside was quiet and I turned to the first problem in the text. I copied it neatly into my notebook, taking the time involved in the writing to sort through the problem. When I finished, the solution was ready to go. The symbols, the equations, the proof, and the deduction flowed seamlessly, working in a clean place in my mind that had not yet been overwhelmed by emotional litter and psychological waste.

Mathematics made for a calm journey. The roadway was always well signed, the destination logically reachable, and the progress predictable. Problem after problem flew by under my fingers, angles and hypotenuse making perfect sense under an umbrella of well organized theorems and their corollary cousins. The time passed, the logic continued, and the calm rippled outward from that one small place inside to other places more troubled and chaotic.

The time flew, my bottom side fell asleep on the hard chair, the sun set, and the light grew dim. I continued as long as there were problems to do, even though I had finished the homework part of it hours before.

Here in this place, I could not only be right rather than right or wrong depending on the mood of the moment, but I could also find a life here that was incredibly calm. I held onto that calm for as long as I could, assisted by the symbols and the theorems on the printed page before me. Math was calm, a world where emotions cast away in favor of order and logic. It was my kind of predictable place... calm and cool as a field of cucumbers.

On my lucky days, there would be no interruption to my time with the math and after hours with the problems, I would crawl into bed, tired and worn out. There, I would sleep both dreamless and calm.

The Determination

I was now in high school and using The Calm over and over again to keep the emotional roller coaster at bay. It was the summer after my freshman year. Another summer to manage the loneliness that would have been all too happy to swallow me up if I let it flow unbounded.

When school ended, the panic began. It started slowly at first, then threatening more as the long, unoccupied days wore on. Unlike when I was younger, I was determined now to thwart both of the Emotion Monsters .... Loneliness and Boredom ... and to keep their ugliness away from me.

On the first day after school's end, I awoke to see the one monster huddled in one corner of my bedroom and the other monster huddled in another. During that first week after school ended, my monsters usually kept their distance as I was still recovering sleep from my typical school day routine. It was a routine that went from 6:45 in the morning to 12 or 1 in the morning ... busy and intentionally full. My two Monsters had no opportunity to jump into my school day. When the summer came though, the Monsters would try again.

For the first week after the school year ended, I slept, spending my brief waking time walking or reading, reasonably content as the two Monsters kept their distance, deep in the corners of my room. Toward the end of that blessedly peaceful first week though, the monsters shifted. They sensed opportunity and started to make noises, once again staging their demand for my spirit.

As in the years before, I kept after the Monsters, matching strategy for strategy to keep them at bay, ceding carefully organized strategies to their haphazard chaotic hunger for my soul. I was smarter now; Little Adult was doing quite well and I spent many days, matching step for step against Loneliness and Boredom. But in the heat of battle against the one Monster, I often lost ground with the other. Switching back and forth between them was draining. Oh so often, the battle was bigger than I was.

I added strategies to those of previous summers with new tricks, every chance I could. Going to the beach was always a big boost; swimming and dancing in the waves released my full spirit in a place, both wild and gentle, where it was safe. Television moved down the list of choices because it was too passive to keep my mind from yielding to the Monsters. Once a week, I busied myself cleaning the entire house which took almost a day and often made Mother happy, a two-for-one deal as far as I was concerned. Whenever I was allowed, I biked over to my best friend's house and enjoyed beyond proportion, an afternoon of talking, watching soap operas, and eating tuna fish sandwiches. Many days, these things worked and the Monsters stayed at bay.

Often, late in the afternoon, I ran out of strategy and there was trouble with Loneliness and Boredom. In one of those key moments of this endless battle, I happened to re-discover some thievery that I had indulged in during my first year of high school. The textbook for my next year of math had mysteriously walked from the classroom, out the door, onto the bus, and into this house. I had done little to stop it. So now, it sat on my book shelf, untouched for the first weeks of summer vacation.

Until, on a particularly lonely day in the heat and humidity of the charming Florida summer, I pulled that very textbook out and curled up on Mother's bed (she was out for the evening). With the TV on, I skimmed the first chapter and to my delight, realized that I didn't have to do a lot of reading to learn how to do the problems. What's more, I didn't need the teacher to do them. Hmm ... this could be a gold mine!

That night and many nights thereafter, I sat on the bed, the TV droning but unattended, and completed problems in the book. One chapter after the other, I lapped up Advanced Algebra, checking the answers in the back of the book and organizing my papers as if indeed I were still in school. Such spontaneous intellectual activity set off a stream of endorphins which did not go unnoticed by Little Adult. It was an "Ah-hah" moment that had major implications for the future.

As the summer went by, a good day saw the morning pass at the beach and late afternoon pass with the math textbook. Other intellectual stimulation joined the math problems. I threw away my Harlequin romance phase and started to read the classics, where the complexity of the writing and the depth of the plots and character development challenged my mind and drew me away from all things present.

Needless to say, the Monsters were altogether not impressed with my new discovery. They still had their time with me when I sat defenseless, depleted, or both, but they didn't have nearly the opportunities they did before. They were losing and I was winning. Ha!

By the time the new school year rolled around, I had finished all the chapters in the algebra book, each set of problems neatly placed in my notebook, and had completed with sincerity, classics that included War and Peace and the Grapes of Wrath. It took me many weeks to admit to my teacher my little adventure with the Advanced Algebra book. She reacted with remarkable calm, gave me a final exam, and pushed me forward a year in math. Onward I went into adventures with trigonometry.

I never did admit to reading War and Peace. I didn't have THAT much courage.

Strategy

I had four simple tricks to survive: deflect, analyze, talk, and tuck. When Mother's criticism came my way, I deflected it with humor and sarcasm at a level carefully engineered to stay off her radar screen. Mother might often suspect that I was responding less than seriously to her tirades, but I was rarely caught and punished for it. When deflecting didn't work, I analyzed. I separated Mother's barbs into categories of Impossible, Unlikely, and Vulnerable. The ones in the Impossible category (like "whore", "sneaky", and "liar") were treated with the "Hurt, cry, but don't waste any more time thinking about it" strategy. The Unlikely and the Vulnerable remarks were harder to handle. They usually involved the Talk strategy ... to friends, to the ocean, to myself, to the piece of paper in my journal. Talk until it hurt less and then Unlikely and Vulnerable could be tucked away somewhere to confront later, when I was no longer living in the house where Mother allowed me to sleep.

But now that I was called a whore, it was getting harder to find a way out of this place, even with the four tricks. Logic didn't matter all that much in this crazy world. No one had to justify what Mother said. Because it was said, it is. A lie, once told often enough, becomes true. I had to figure out what to do with these once lies ... but now 'truths'.

Before I became a whore, the plan as Mother also once or twice said was to hook a rich man and marry him. That way, I would have money and through money, I would have a life worth living. I would also be happy.

But now we had a problem. Who would marry a whore? None of the rich kids at school nor even the middle class kids had a mom who was a whore. Television, romance novels, and even the classics confirmed it. No whore had a life beyond the seedy, drug-infested corners of the inner city. Some burned out young, sinking even further. Or they dove headlong into drugs themselves, losing all opportunity for scratching out a better life. Or they simply hardened, and became the managers of other whores. That's what the stories around me said and for a while I merged with their reality, defeated and hopeless.

An unlikely candidate for a rescue from my dilemma, Hollywood arrived with some useful inspiration. A movie called 'Angel' was released in the middle of my thrashing hopelessness, I saw it at the local drive-in during its short-lived showing. The main character, an attractive and innocent young lady, was of the same economic class as me. She, like me, was rather desperate to be upwardly mobile and decided that a college education could be precisely the ticket out of her situation. With the help of others including a benevolent rendition of a pimp, Angel devised a scheme by which she would sell her body to pay her tuition bill. The income flowed, college materialized, and Angel moved onward and upward. Indeed, Hollywood had almost managed to romanticize prostitution in the name of higher education.

Here would be the place where the reader might think that I, the naive young teenager, would start to hatch plans to prostitute myself on the streets of the city to pay for college. Not that simple. Or stupid, thank you.

Three things hatched instead. First, I realized that no matter what the price, I was going to leave this place. Whether I was a whore or just thought I was one didn't matter. Healing meant leaving and leaving meant resources. If those resources meant borderline or illegal activity, then so be it. It was just a matter of picking the resources most likely to land me in college and least likely to land me in jail.

I also now realized what being born in America meant. The fine print in the American Dream told me that the chances of me having to resort to illegal or immoral activity to get into university were rather small. Based on the fine print, I began to understand that the American Dream might also apply to someone as worthless and lost as I. My resolve to go to college, formerly waffling in the wind, now became etched in concrete.

I also saw now that there was no way to romanticize prostitution. Reducing my body to a source of income would destroy some part of me that even all of Mother's words and choices couldn't take away. From one (rather low quality) movie called 'Angel', there sprang a seed of visceral resistance to prostitution and its cousins promiscuity and rape. Too immature to know what it was all about, I just let the seed sit inside of me and germinate. Someday a long time from now, it would grow into a healthy sexuality.

Imagine that.

It gave a whole new importance to College Bound.

Tools of the Body

Our bodies are our gardens -- our wills are our gardeners

William Shakespeare

Walking

Sometimes, the sadness inside of me was so acute that the only way to release it was to cry ... sobbing until the edge rolled off the pain and I could breathe again. Other times, the sadness was more like a blanket stitched in lead, weighing so heavy on me that it was hard to get up. From the leaden state, it was impossible to go dashing into a round of boisterous exercise or even into a conversation with a girlfriend to get much needed relief. Instead, I could only do the closest thing to sitting around, doing nothing... walking around and doing next to nothing.

It was usually warm, so I was saved the added burden of suiting up... jacket, hat, boots... whatever those folks up north did to be able to walk out the door. Instead, I waited for Mother to be gone or otherwise occupied, slipped on some sandals, and quietly slid out the door. From there, it didn't much matter which way I went. One foot in front of the other... took me wherever they may. Me and my feet, we walked .... focused on little more than each step, each cycle of my legs rolling smoothly through a respective hip joint.

At first, it was always so hard. The sadness weighed every muscle down and simply walking might have well been running a marathon. But gradually, as each step gave way to the next, and the distance between here and the house grew longer, it became ever slightly easier. I might just walk around the block or I might walk for miles without pausing. But I always walked until it didn't hurt anymore, never turning around until the heavy blanket of despair was cast to the side.

After a fraction of a mile or many miles behind me, whether on pavement, grass, or sand, I would turn back the other way. My steps were always lighter on the return. No longer running a marathon but effortlessly engaging in motion, my thoughts would also effortlessly move beyond the simple task of walking and go to a different place. On the return, I would daydream so deeply that I lost track of where I was, often landing me back at the house well after dark... and squarely back into a spot of trouble with Mother. It was well worth it.

Walk until it no longer hurts.

Return on a lightness of heart.

Peace

There were certain things that stopped Mother's anger... not many, but there were a few. All were welcome.

Sickness (mine, not hers) was one of such things. Now, there was a certain matter of rules to the sickness, mind you. It had to be real, complete with obvious misery and a bonafide fever of over one hundred degrees. Without these basic things, it failed to defuse Mother's anger. So when my fevers came, I coddled them into steamy wonders, making sure I could pass The 100 degree Test. When I was younger, these fevers had been pure torture. Now, they were pure opportunity.

One day during school, I could tell by early in the fifth period in history class that my pure opportunity lurked nearby. By the time of my favorite class (trigonometry), my head nodded and my concentration wandered. My forehead was hot and my skin flushed pink. Leaving school early was not an option because there was no one to come get me. But finally, the last class period of the day crawled by, the last bell rang, and I stumbled slowly home, via the waiting school bus.

At home, I bunched blankets together, tucked multiple pillows behind my back and head, and created a quasi-cocoon for myself. I helped myself to a glass of juice and crawled inside my constructed cocoon. The ache in my muscles comes to rest, the world grows quiet around me, and Mother even offers a concerned smile after her hand on my forehead convinces her that I have triumphantly passed The 100 degree Test.

I could go hours like this now, at peace... warm and quiet with no craziness as I fake napping in my comfortable cocoon while sneaking enough glances at the television to follow the plot of whatever sitcom happened to be broadcasting into the room.

Here was a peace that was so large, so unusual, so welcome that the discomfort of flu or cold or other virus was no match for it. I loved my cocoon, almost so much that I wished I would never get well. But invariably, I did (get well) ... whether after 24 hours or a few days. The peace always refreshed and healed in its own way, so I could walk out into the world able to withstand another round of the craziness with Mother with just a little bit more grace and strength.

The peace offered one more successful step forward ... toward and away and ... out of this place.

Dancing

The morning rumbled with discontent. I didn't get up on time. I wasn't wearing the right clothes. I wasn't eating the best food for breakfast nor the correct amount of it. I wasn't using the utensils the right way. I was stupid one minute and a slob the next. Mother saw nothing right in me. And this morning, I followed suit. I saw nothing right in me either.

It was a school holiday for me and a work day for Mother, so later rather than sooner, Mother left the house for work. She left a few strongly worded rules in her wake that came with consequences I would surely avoid. As her car pulled out of the driveway, the rules closed in on my space, leaving me restricted to the house with limited phone privileges for the day. Another exciting day in crazy-dise.

I watched the car head down the street and turn left onto the next road. I waited ten or fifteen minutes to see if there would be any return trips to check on my behavior. I waited another five, curled up on the couch, trying to shift gears from the hopeless to the hopeful.

After a half an hour had passed, the risk of a returning Mother sighting had also passed. I crawled off the couch and pulled the old, beat-up transistor radio out of my room. I pulled up the antenna, careful not to yank too hard and permanently disconnect my only tether to the world of music. I put the radio on the window sill, in the sweet spot that I knew would give me the very best reception. Slowly, I turned the volume knob until I heard the familiar click as the radio went from off to on. The volume, weak and full of static at first, gradually improved, rising to a level that put at risk all the lonely bunnies that were now crowding into the corners of the small living room. After an irritating sequence of commercials, the garden variety popular music began. This one was one of my favorites.... a song called Walking on Sunshine.

I forgot about the sunshine outside that I was forbidden to enjoy today. I forgot about the parade of criticism that started the morning out less than right. Sitting on the couch, I closed my eyes and felt the quick tempo synch with the upbeat lyrics. The tempo called my feet and my feet called my spirit and the whole package of me was suddenly upright. I twirled round and round, arms in motion, feet moving faster and faster. Dancing .... twirling ... walking on sunshine. It's bound to feel good!

I twirled some more ... bounced across the floor... then a few more times to come to a spinning stop on the couch as the song came to a close. There, I giggled then giggled some more, just as a well adjusted child would.

and indeed I could too.

Tools of the Heart

Therefore, we do not lose heart. Though outwardly we are wasting away, yet inwardly we are being renewed day by day ... So we fix our eyes not on what is seen but on what is unseen.

2 Corinthians 4:16-15:8

Serenity

There was always something about warm sunshine that fixed almost everything. Lucky me, I was almost always guaranteed a generous dose of it between two and three on a school day afternoon, when the ever reliable school bus dropped me off near the house where Mother allowed me to sleep.

Whether I arrived to school on time on the occasional uneventful morning or whether I was late after yet another round of insults from Mother... whether school was boring or frustrating, whether I attended class or not, I almost always landed on the school bus at the end of the day. By myself on a long green seat, I did my best to shrink into as small a package as possible, avoiding another round of senseless ridicule from my adolescent bus mates. It's as if the other teens smelled the ridicule from Mother on my clothes and felt compelled to add to it. Such are the kind hearts of teenagers.

Shrinking into my seat usually works and when the door opened at my stop, I am slow to gather my things so I can be sure to be the last off the bus. The others will walk on ahead and promptly forget about me. All works according to plan and I am now here, standing on this spot on a dirt road alone, gathering my school books into a comfortable position. Assembled, I will start the walk home soon. It is quiet now, because the other kids are long gone. The sunshine is beaming in from the west to my left, warming my bare shoulders and casting a light into my eyes that could sometimes be confused for something coming from within. Before I start to walk, I will close my eyes, standing still and inhaling deeply, forcing my incoming breath to corner and contain my frustration and anguish, my loneliness, and my pain.

Thus cornered, I can now exhale that package of toxin. Another deep breath will now fill me with what is peaceful and innocent in the warm and quiet afternoon sunshine. Now stepping forward, my insides temporarily free of darkness, I am strolling through a gateway of serenity. The sun dapples through the trees, playing with the now half smile growing on my face. Each step reminds me now that there must surely be serene roads to walk in this life.

I am in no hurry to get home. Although the school books in my arms grow heavier, my steps grow lighter as I pass one block and then the next. While I am crossing the street, one of the neighbors sees me passing by in this sheltered state and will later tell Mother what a serene daughter she has raised. Sigh. Serenity possessed but not begotten in the way the neighbor imagines.

I am off in my own little secure and serene world. I wish that I could walk like this forever. But now, I've reached the driveway. The serenity, not forgotten, dances nearby and reassures me that she will return after the next school bus. Replacing her, the knot in my stomach has returned, sneering at serenity surrounding.

I walk in the door, rejuvenated but tense, almost prepared for another evening in this place where Mother allows me to sleep.

Passion

With every step, my toes disappeared under the white sand, attached to feet that were all too happy to have divested themselves of shoes. Today, those crafty feet had biked all the way down here to the beach and the shoes had been a necessary evil. The six miles from the place where Mother allowed me to live and this place here in the sand were not the easiest to negotiate. The roads would not see bike lanes for years to come, much less drivers who respected bicyclists alongside. In spite of these small obstacles, my feet and I had survived another helmet-free escapade along the streets of the small city. That escapade had started early this morning when ...

I woke up with a fire blazing in my heart that had nowhere to burn and nowhere to go. Expressions of passion around Mother usually led to ridicule, long speeches, or other wet blanket approaches to parenting. So, I locked passion tightly away inside of me, awaiting some moment in the far future when I presumed it would become OK to be whole again.

Stubborn as that passion could be, in the night, it had leaked out of its tightly guarded corner in my heart. Fire leapt into my eyes, my expression, demanding a brighter and sunnier place in the emotional landscape of my life. Before it could be discovered by the in-house emotions archaeologist, otherwise known as Mother, I hopped onto my bicycle and dashed away.

Now out of breath and sweating profusely in the hot Florida sun, I take another step out onto the sand, close my eyes, and breathe deeply. In the exhale, passion and its cousin hope rose to the surface of me. Passion out of its box had no intention of quietly returning to its place and when I finally opened my eyes, long breath exhaled, I let go what needed to burn.

Toes still buried, warming in the sun-drenched sand, I was now standing between two small sand dunes with sea oat grasses reaching to the sky on both sides and the vast blue expanse of the ocean directly in front of my fresh eyes. I started to run as fast as one can on a sandy beach, stumbling sometimes as my feet occasionally sank far more than expected into the thick sand. I felt the hotness of the sand, growing more intense with each stride. My feet, now approaching uncomfortably hot, eagerly sought that delicate line between the dry, hot white sand and the firm, wet, cool sand that marked the beginning of the surf. I was losing patience for the cool relief of the ocean water and I pushed for faster and further. My thighs were already burning from the long bike ride and now the tension climbed one more notch in my already tight muscles.

Ahhh... there it was. My feet hit the surf, creating a big splash from my crazy sprint that both cooled my tender feet and soothed the aching muscles along my legs. The waves rolled in, taking away all the physical discomfort I had managed to accumulate from there to here. Ahhh.... it was better than any spa anywhere.

As the waves rolled in and then back out again, my passion rolled out with them, entering into a dance that knew nothing of oppression or despair. I now ran along the break line, where the smooth curl of the waves continued to collapse under its own weight into a stunning scroll of white. I jumped over one small breaker and then another, then a larger, then an even larger. I jumped until I couldn't jump any higher and collapsed into the surf, laughing as another wave broke over my head, cooling the entire rest of me down to something close to normal body temperature. I ran again, playing hard to get between breaking wave and breaking wave. The waves played along as if they knew the rules of my wildly impulsive game. I ran until my lungs ached, until all I could do was sit in the wet sand, waves rolling over me ... one, two, three.

The ocean had her vast passion that was graciously spread out unending before me. She spoke to my own heart whose passion, though not as indomitable, made its own private connection to the salty sea. MyOcean turned what was left in my heart into exuberant life energy that would not, could not disappear.

The ocean broke yet another wave over my tired body. I laughed at her and rolled over, content and full of life, as if nothing bad had ever happened in the history of me.

Tools of the Spirit

It is the Spirit who gives life
the flesh profits nothing.

John 6:63

More Ocean

MyOcean was a place for my passion, a fun and playful romp that never failed to turn dark to light and heaviness to weightlessness in my troubled struggling heart. I returned to my isolated relationship with MyOcean often, no matter what time of year or what the state of the house where Mother allowed me to sleep. Just as I thought MyOcean, full of fun and play, could offer no more, she surprised me once again.

I had taken to the habit of walking to the edge of the Sound every evening at sunset. The Sound was a calm, peaceful stretch of water separated from the open Gulf only by a barrier island that was more and more sprinkled with commercialized condominium fare. Shortly after leaving the house, just far enough to be out of sight, I stash my shoes, nuisance item that they are, under the nearest shrub. I love the feeling of the grass, the sand, and the barnacled rocks under the toughened soles of my feet. I walk along the rocks in the water, well enough away from other evening strollers that I can find isolation and peace, a suitable end to many a chaotic day. I walk and walk along those rocks, attention consumed by avoiding the sharpest of the barnacles, those that would cause even my seasoned feet to wince. My trek along the rocks would leave me at the start of a broken-down pier that had its heyday long before I discovered the rocks and this walk. Ignoring the No Trespassing and the Condemned signage except to climb over its dilapidated structure, I walk light-footed along the remaining boards, oblivious to injury or risk as most adolescents are. At the end of the pier, under a gazebo of sorts, one that was equally likely to cave in on me as the rest of this decaying structure, I sit, perched on one of the few remaining boards capable of carrying my weight. My back lays against a beam of marginal stability. Ignoring the precariousness of my position, I turn to see only the ocean, the waves, and the birds searching for their evening meal upon the water. The sun is moving toward the horizon, bidding its goodbye for the day. This nightly routine continues regardless of what the cycle with Mother looks like. It comforts me. It gives me peace.

One day, something very different falls into this scene. It goes well beyond the peace created by the brilliant splash of sunset color and the entertaining flocks of shore birds. On that special day, as I sit, eyes partially closed, reconnecting with the peace and the passion that MyOcean represents, a strong vibrant energy approaches me from the direction of the oncoming sunset. It compels me, draws me to face it. My eyes open wide.

There are really no words to say how I know that this is God, no visual description that can convey the shocking depth of the moment. But indeed, it is Him. I have no doubt. In that moment, between sunset and dusk, God very simply approaches me from across the water.

He desires to speak to me. I don't know Him. All I have heard in a decade and a half of life about Him is typically His name used in a moment of anger, laced around profanity. I don't even have the question on my mind: Who is this God? God is not offended by what I know and what I don't know. He comes anyway.

He starts by showing me a small bottle, filled to the brim with a clear liquid. He directs my gaze around and beyond Him where many of these bottles lie clustered on a light-filled shelf. He tells me that He has counted every drop in each bottle, more than once. Then, He tells me they are my tears. And He waits, as I sit there in the palm of His hand trying to understand this overwhelming love. For a moment, I think it is just my imagination working overtime, but this moment of doubt passes so quickly I barely remember it being there in the first place.

In that single sunset, I became no longer alone in this world. I stopped being one who had no direction, no place to go. A single sunset. A changed Life.

After this day, MyOcean would become more than just a place to visit. She would become a haven to meditate, to listen for God. She would become a friend whose heart and mine became readily intertwined.

MyOcean was not always required to be nice, as any busy hurricane season would attest, but she always called to me when I came to her. Beyond her own call, I would now also hear the call of an all loving heavenly Father. With every passing wave and every setting sun, I would know that He was present and powerful, always offering the palm of His hand to my longing heart.

A Little Bit of Miracle

Sometime not so long after the sunset during which God found me, a little miracle walked my way. It was a spring day and I was wearing shorts, acclimating to the ever increasing temperatures that were the tropical Florida repertoire in the brief cool spring. The mailman came the same time as he always did on Saturdays, a few hours later than his weekday stop, likely a delay due to some unseen change in schedule, businesses to be skipped, store fronts to be passed ... until Monday rolled around again and reinstated his normal routine.

When I opened the mailbox, the plain brown envelope didn't really say much about the letter and the T-shirt inside. But when I saw the return address (from MIT), my heart skipped a beat and a million or more butterflies took flight in my stomach. I took the envelope into my room, trying to avoid Mother along my way. I opened it up and read the lovely letter crafted on attractive ivory and red letterhead.

At first, I reacted in a calm and organized way, taking the time to pull the fresh cotton T-shirt out of its plastic bag and unfolding it with some care to avoid wrinkling the acceptance letter which announced its arrival. I finished unfolding the T-shirt and chuckled that it was a long-sleeve variety which was, of course, not particularly wearable as the temperatures were already flirting with 90. I had no idea that Women at MIT (as the T-shirt proclaimed) could be a bad thing. I had not a single clue that being a woman was going to make a bit of a difference or be more difficult than being a man as an engineer. I was delightfully oblivious to all the implications of the gender gap.

As I read the letter again, my spirit, unwilling to be boxed any longer, burst out of its carefully controlled place. Without thinking (which was precisely my error), I ran to Mother, jumping up and down with the T-shirt in one hand and the letter in the other. I handed it to her, all the while repeating Guess what? Guess what? As if every molecule in the room hadn't heard me the first time I said it.

As I bounced up and down on the cool linoleum lining the kitchen floor, I didn't even see the words coming, the ones that would stop by excitement cold. Mother's eyes were that icy blue now. She interrupted and said:

"I don't know what you're so excited about; there is no way you'll find enough money to go there (MIT)."

And away my spirit went. My excitement, the wind in my sails, and the light in my eyes just disappeared as quickly as they had come. Ugly words, as so often before, were now made even more damaging by my lowered defenses. I closed my eyes and tried to stem the tears for just long enough to retreat back to my room.

In the days that follow, I am flattened by the financial dilemma of going to college. The less expensive schools in my home state demand the same amount of money from the "Parents send your check here" funds as the Ivy League schools. The financial aid forms, the scholarships, and the people who decided such things all naturally assumed that the parents would contribute to the best of their ability. The difference between the in-state public schools and the out-of-state elite schools is that the latter have an additional clause called "Parents cosign the loan here" that confounds the problem even further.

So I settle into believing that I won't go to college after all. I resign myself to the local community college for which I already have a full scholarship. I grow convinced that the local community college is all that someone like me can expect. I shouldn't complain. Yet, at the back of my mind, I recognize the danger of continuing to live at home after high school is finished. I know that my determination has some end out there and my resilience will run into hard limits. Eventually, some critical word, a well timed insult, or a perfect storm of abuse at some future time could break me. I am desperate to leave this town, this place, and be far away from the house where Mother allows me to sleep.

One day during history class, mind wandering as usual, I am pondering the limited choices before me. I am trying to devise a creative plan for attending the best state university which is 150 miles away. A student walks into the class, hall pass in hand, and gives it to the teacher. Shortly thereafter, I hear my name, get up out of my reverie and my chair at the exact same moment, and take the pass from the teacher's hand, heading off to the front office to see what this particular summons is all about. I close the classroom door behind me, not all that disappointed that history and I have parted for the day.

Seated now in my guidance counselor's office, I fill her in on my limited choices for post-secondary education. Somewhere in my summary of the choices I had in front of me, I must have mentioned Mother's reaction to the acceptance letter from MIT but it never occurred to me that my counselor would actually listen to me. When she said "Accept the offer from MIT, turn the rest down", I stared at her as if she had just landed in her office, courtesy of some spaceship visiting from a far-off planet. She gave me some reason why it wouldn't hurt to accept the offer from MIT. After all, the worst that could happen is that I would have to work for a year before going to college. OK, maybe that was true. Still, it was such a risk.

I accepted the offer. With limited professional skills and all I could muster from a first course in typing, I wrote my very first business letter to MIT to say that I would come in the fall. I also thanked them for offering someone like me a chance to move up in the world. I hated the hope that was rising up inside of me when I wrote the letter. I was sure that another crushing disappointment was not very far away at all.

A few weeks later, the same guidance counselor summoned me to her office once again. I thought little of it, although I was confused as to why I was being denied scholarship after scholarship, despite my top-of-the-class academic record. I just assumed that those people who decided on scholarships didn't think someone like me was worth it, no matter what my grades.

Imagine my shock then when my counselor, bless her guardian angel heart, began to describe the $60,000 scholarship that was now mine. The only requirement for accepting the scholarship was that I attend a school that allowed me to spend it all.

So much for the state university idea. MIT, here I come.

I laughed at her. I just laughed and laughed again. I couldn't imagine and had not even dared to think I would ever run across a miracle in the chaos. But, like miracles so often do, this one just showed up on my lap, with no warning, no logic, and no bounds. After I stopped laughing, I immediately started crying. They were long sobbing tears that caused a flood of relief to stream down my face. It went on for quite a while but finally, with red puffy eyes in tow, I returned to class.

By the end of the day, I refused to make the same mistake a second time. I went to the place where Mother allowed me to sleep and pretended as if nothing happened.

Months ago, on the pier during the first time God came and spoke to me, He made me a promise. He told me that it wouldn't always be this way.

Indeed. God keeps His promises. Onward we go.

The day came of course, when I had to tell Mother that I was moving 1500 miles away from this place to start a life that could be different from where it started. Not inclined to tell her alone where she had the opportunity to weave a new way and a new set of words to crush my hopes and dreams, I waited for the annual awards program.

On the big day, she sat far away in the big auditorium in the last few rows, while I sat in front with the other award recipients. I watched and waited, as all my peers received their respective awards. We were seniors and there were many. I waited a long time. Long enough to wonder if it were really true. Long enough to crush my own hope, unwilling to be brutally disappointed again.

Finally, the last announcement of the day came. It was for the child called whore. They called her name and she walked slowly onto the stage. She turned around to look at the audience and first saw Mother sitting far in the back. She then turned slowly to look at the others. They were standing and clapping. She wondered why they were making such a noise.

Surely, they would not be clapping for the little whore.

The child looked for the other person they surely must be applauding. She looked for a long time, but she didn't find any others. They were clapping for her. They had hope for her. They were excited that she was moving on and away.

The tears started to come. The hope exploded in her chest. She ventured a small smile and then a full blown affair, whose light extended well and deep into her eyes.

There was a world out there that cared about the little whore. A world that would allow her to climb out of this place where she started, and now begin the journey of healing and becoming someone else.

Dear Mother

Trust in the Lord with all your heart and lean not on your own understanding; in all your ways acknowledge him and he will make your paths straight.

Proverbs 3:5-6

40 some years after the Beginning

Dear Mother,

I've been doing this relationship with God thing now for over twenty years. It has been the great roller coaster. He has had to chase me up and down, into sin and back out... and this way and that, deep into the broken-ness and back out, creating impossible moments of joy to rise above all the darkness, making it seem as if it never existed. Those joys, brief as they are in my life and now clouded by too many decades of pain and loneliness, have kept the hope alive and let the faith continue to grow, bit by painful bit. Step back, step forward ... Stumble, get up ... and go again.

I know first hand that holding His is the only way out of all this damage toward healing. You often say that my strong faith combined with churchgoing must make for an unhealthy obsession with some cult, making me even more dysfunctional than you. Sigh ... I long for you to find Him and to cast the pain and fear from which those kinds of ideas come from aside. I have hoped beyond hope that you will lay your armor down and just try a few steps along the path with Him. But, instead, you have walked and walked away over these decades, holding fast to anger, protecting the wounds, and mounting the anxiety that now joins up with Satan's favorite playmate, Death.

I am so sad, helpless. I am in way over my head. Years ago, you must have known the cancer was starting to take hold. Through the vomiting and the bleeding, you never said a word to me. I watched you suddenly grow old, all those years ago, and knew something dreadful had started. But I prayed that of all the ways God could plan your path out of this life that He would not choose the way of Cancer. I prayed and prayed for decades that He would choose another way. You always said He would just take you in the night, as you slept. But His plans were never yours ... not then and not now.

Neither are His plans mine. So, now we will have to walk these last steps together. But, I'm not leaving my God behind ... He will come with us, whether you like it or not.

Bless all the goodness that you still harbor inside of you, Mother. Bless you. May Peace come now.

The End

The day draws close
When darkness finally becomes light
When the shadows disappear

She will turn
and come Home

The end of the story begins by ...
Resisting

Mixed here and there in life, we hear stories about how Satan takes advantage of folks when they are vulnerable and afraid.... but hearing about it doesn't at all seem to prepare you for the moments in life when the enemy brazenly delights in exploiting your weaknesses.

I called Mother early this morning and she told me that today, she would die. I asked her if I should come to her from Seattle to Florida. She said it would be senseless.

My sister called shortly after I hung up the phone. Mother was threatening to slit her wrists and throat.

As my sister's words sank in from 3000 miles away, my frustration and fear exploded in me just like the icelandic volcano exploding then, halfway around the world. I was still commuting; it was still rush hour. There were too many cars ... too much pain in my heart. Too many brake lights... too many thoughts zig-zagging in my head. I pulled over. I got out of the car. I screamed. I ranted and raved. Right there, on an impersonal freeway, I melted down. My fellow commuters sped by without slowing... without noticing. Of course. What a cold world it could be.

After the meltdown passed, Mother's neighbor Sol called. Sol had just left Mother's house after sitting with Mother for some time. By the time she left, there was no more talk of knives and slit wrists lingering in the air. Yet Mother's starvation continued. Later, as Mother lay in her house in the sweltering summer heat in Florida denying herself any relief offered from air conditioning, I sat briefly at my desk, breathing in the cool Northwest air floating innocently into my open office window. I felt her pangs of starvation from afar. I had been there. Yet when I had been starving at less than a year old, I was struggling for life. Here and now, Mother was struggling for death. The confusion blossomed and grew inside of me. Then, I put the pangs away, deep inside of me. It was time to work.

The day at the office marched on, as if nothing at all were amiss. Two long and critical graduate student exams fed my endless conflict between staying here in my seemingly normal cocoon for a few more days or heading out to the crisis that was now escalating in Florida. Some of my colleagues insisted on pushing meetings 30 or 40 minutes past their end, despite my pleas to simply end business affairs on time, I spoke of a "family emergency", even described the urgent and imminent suicide threat. But their business remained important enough to hold me to my seat. Their faces remained impassive, their hearts impossibly hard.

In the spaces between meetings, my husband and I both worked the phones to Hospice, doctors, and any medical personnel at all we could persuade to speak with us. Finally, after key conversations with two surprisingly helpful nurses, the fog of decision cleared. Mother was indeed closing in on death. It was time for me to go. Go.

Still I resisted. Scared and tired, I wanted no more part of this tragic and seemingly hopeless battle... not only the physiological battle with oncoming death but the spiritual one that had now raged for over four decades, staging good against evil across a landscape of unending anxiety and drama.

Much, much later... sometime in the afternoon, I finally pressed the override switch, the one inside my brain marked "Go anyway". Half asleep, feeling like a truck had rolled right over me, I managed, after some comic missteps, to click the correct buttons on my computer screen and Delta Airlines kindly coughed up an air ticket for me.

Satan tossed my fear around like a seal with a ball today, delighting in my impatience with my colleagues, in my overcommitted time, and most, the very most of all... in my fear of what was now to come.

Flying Away

By the next morning, a Thursday, Satan had been kicked out the door again, thanks in no small part to the faith and wisdom of my husband John who knows how to deal with such things. By 1 p.m., I was on an airplane. By 2 p.m., I was still on a plane that hadn't moved yet. By 3 p.m., the plane was moving but my brain wasn't. By 4 p.m., my brain was moving and I realized I was in trouble with my 1 hour connection time in my midwest stopover city.

I was shy and tempted to not say a single word to the flight attendants about my dilemma. Too many times in the past, I had seen the passenger's concern and anxiety be dismissed by airlines and airline employees tossed about in impossible budget conditions. This time, however, I kicked myself and eased out of my seat. Stepping to the back of the airplane, I began to explain my situation to the flight attendant.

There in the back of the plane, some 30,000 feet above the midwest, came the first miracle of this long journey. The first flight attendant told me not to worry. The second helped to move me to a seat that allowed me to be first off the airplane. The third made the call to hold the next flight. The fourth helped me with my bags. Last but absolutely not least, the lead flight attendant, the first one I had poured out my heart to, gave me a strong warm hug. Amazing really. God could even get through to the seemingly impenetrable corporate wall of the american airline industry!

Now, on the second flight, the time sped by quickly. As the airplane prepared for landing, the warmth brought on by the familiarity of the flat Florida landscape below intersected the equally familiar fear of the anxiety and strain forever associated with interacting with Mother. I closed my eyes, prayed another of countless prayers, and took a deep breath.

As I had done dozens of times as an adult, I walked off the airplane in Tampa and entered the satellite terminal, taking some comfort in the familiar surroundings. Exiting into the main terminal, however, I again couldn't contain my emotions and melted down right in the middle of the concourse. It was almost midnight before I recovered from a long bout of uncontrollable sobs and all too frequent moments of total despair. I dragged myself to the rental car counter. By then, my eyes were so puffy & red, my countenance so pathetic, that even the rental car agents went light on their add-on sales pitches.

Three Days of Despair

I wouldn't write, could barely sleep, and struggled to eat. At first, I felt shocked: "This is not happening,"

Then, I saw the coming train wreck. All of the choices at hand were awful. Not unlike the first eighteen years of my life here in this community, living in the house where Mother allowed me to sleep. Shock, panic, fear ... and then despair.

This familiar cycle of our lives together, Mother's life and my own, now started again for the very last time.

Not Happening

When I finally arrived at the neighbor Sol's house at 1 a.m. in the morning on Friday, I walked over to Mother's house; the door was now unlocked 24 hours a day because Mother could no longer walk or move from the couch that was tucked away against the far wall in the small living room. When I walked in the door, the skeletal look that had shocked me a few weeks earlier no longer had any effect. I didn't want to believe what was happening, so I pretended it wasn't. I remained oblivious to the flags of impending death.

How could I possibly ignore the crystal clear message embedded in this hot humid room, with urine wafting in powerful waves from the couch where Mother now had lost control of her bodily functions? I could. So I did.

I walked in, I sat down, I talked, I listened, I waited, I absorbed.... I left, I paced, I lay down, I paced, I lay down again, and I rested... sort of.

I now tried to Accept it for What it Was. What it was is this:

Every thirty minutes like clockwork, Mother asks for her ice cold bottle of water from the refrigerator. After gulping several swallows, she rolls over on her side, at the edge of the couch, and drops her head into the small bathroom size garbage can sitting nearby. She throws up the water and some bizarre almost impossible stomach contents. She grabs a pre-folded series of multiple sheets of toilet paper, wipes her mouth, tosses the paper, and rolls back to her original position on her back. She tries to sleep. Her body doesn't allow it. She suffers.

One night, in the hours well past midnight when, as usual, I am unable to sleep, I will wander back across the street from Sol's house and slip in the door, hoping that Mother will now be sleeping peacefully. Instead, awake, she turns her head slightly. I ask if she would like me to stay. She nods.

I pull out the mattress from the other bedroom, drag it across the hardwood floor, and lay it in the living room. I lay there, carefully watching her breathe, praying and trying to breathe myself. She will wake me every 30 minutes for her water. I will sleep fitfully but will get up in the morning and return to my bed at Sol's house for a little bit more sleep.

The next night, I try the same again. It is easy to give Mother comfort now. There are no angry words coming my way from Mother's mouth, only angry looks from her eyes. These are manageable. As the night before, I am awake for a very long time, finally falling fast asleep in the late hours of the night. An hour passes. I wake. I am eye to eye with an oversized palmetto bug. He stares at me, mocking me... as if he knows how many of his kind taunted me in childhood. The terror returns. I must go. I give Mother one more sip of water and leave, knowing I have disappointed her. Across the street, I toss, turn, and go nowhere with my thoughts and everywhere with my feelings.

In the morning, I am tired. My sister Mary would like me to do a few more things. I snap at her. She snaps back. She leaves. It is no one's fault, but we each want to believe otherwise.

Now, with no more help from Mary, the demands grow. It is too much. It's time to break away. Only for a little while.

I am in the rental car. I drive away, searching for familiar comforts. At Starbucks, I order my favorite hot drink even though every sane person around me is ordering iced drinks in the heat. Leaving with that all familiar comforting coffee in hand, I am now searching for a pool, a place to swim, a time for things to be normal, to feel that comforting stretch of my body gliding through the yielding water. The pool is, surprisingly, where Mapquest said it was. Thunderheads lurk nearby and my window of opportunity in the outdoor pool is slim. I slip quickly into my bathing suit and dash into the cool water. I am the only person in a huge pool that would be otherwise filled with laughing families and joyful play. I bask in the peace, close my eyes ...

The sun had not made an appearance since I touched down in Tampa. As I stroke through the clear blue water, the sudden light on my eyelids doesn't register. As I turn at the edge of the pool, I reluctantly open my eyes, daring to take a peak at the world beyond. To my delight, the thunderheads have gone and the sun is now lighting up a wet and humid world around me. The palm trees, the hibiscus, all that is living and photosynthesizing, perks up in the glow. I turn my head toward the sun that is now low in the sky, smile, and start stroking across the water again. As was the case so many times in my early years here, the sun, the water, and the calm are for now my whole world, the only pieces of my reality I need to be concerned with.

God has my attention. Over the years, He has developed His own special language with me, through certain animals and certain cues... all conveyed to me as I observe the world around me. Trained as a scientist to observe and be ever watchful, God has taken advantage of my heavily trained senses and communicates with me by using them to capture my attention when my endless spinning mind might otherwise ignore what He longs for me to hear.

One of His cues now appears in the sky above me. Contrary to their prescribed course of existing, a flock of great blue herons, at least six in total, now fly across the sky above me. Solitary and independent birds by nature, the great blue heron simply doesn't hang out with others of its kind. But, for today, God has changed the rules, if simply to let me know that He is nearby. I watch overhead, as the unlikely flock circles once, then twice, then finally heads off into the horizon. Peace settles back over me. The all-loving, endearing God touches my hand and the world around me grows increasingly calmer, soothing my troubled and tired heart.

Finally finishing my swim after some more gawking at the sky above, I take a moment poolside to enjoy the warm sun on my skin, to thank God for His endearing blessing, to bask in the renewed hope and strength in my heart, and to share with my husband by phone yet another small miracle along this dark path.

In the car again, now driving, I am still in my bathing suit, comfortable and cool in this steamy tropical summer climate. It is just a few hours since I left, but I feel like a new person, ready to go back into this struggle with Mother, to serve and be alongside however I can.

Train Wreck

But now back at the house, the couch is soaked even more with urine. Sol and I struggle to change it, to put plastic where the soaking might otherwise be. My husband John is shocked that we are not using gloves. We switch to wearing gloves, but Mother is saddened by this. She thinks that we are treating her as second class, as an inferior. We have no choice. The urine and bodily fluid continue to come, completely contrary to the fact that no fluid of any substance is being absorbed or digested. The couch gets wetter, the smell stronger. Mother is so hard to lift; I am afraid that I will break something as my hands touch almost nothing more than bones.

The weather has returned to being mercifully overcast and rainy, keeping the temperatures in the 80's rather than the steamy, unbearable 90's. Mother's house has no air conditioning. The thunderstorms come every day. They sound angry. When the fireworks join them on the fourth of July, the noise and the chaos rage against the struggle, tormenting the wait that goes on in the hot humid house where Mother lays.

Sol and I are weary, leaning on each other, with few answers and even fewer solutions. We are only coping, step by step, aware that as Mother gets weaker, we are not enough here. I call nurse after nurse, healthcare company after hospital. No one will come without doctor's referral, Mother's consent, or both. And neither are likely. Mother is too afraid to trust others with these last days.

The phone calls go on. The strategy conversations with Sol roll over, one into the other. Many things are discussed many times over. Mother continues to insist: no doctors, no hospice, no nurses. She only wants Sol and I, but we are very, very clearly not enough for what is needed here.

The next day, I make another desperate cell phone call, this time in the middle of the street -- the only place where my cell phone can get a reasonable signal. Here, in the middle of the street, I can hear my husband on the other end of the line. I can see the choices ... and it is time to have a more serious, inconsolable meltdown.

Such was my ruckus while melting down in the middle of the street that Sol came out and pulled me back to her house for comfort and a reset. Sobbing, sniffling, sobbing more, and finally depletion -- a last sniffle and then calm.

In the calm after the meltdown, all the choices before Sol and Mother and I, limited as they were, lined up.

Choices

Choice #1: We could continue as we were. Honoring Mother's desire to have nothing to do with those she didn't know, including doctors, hospitals, nurses, and hospice. We could struggle, in a myriad of bodily fluids, to turn Mother over, to try to keep her dry to the extent that she would allow. I could just cry harder as I attempted to lift her, apologizing all the way for not being strong enough to care for her in these last days. We could just continue the unavoidable contact with bodily fluid ... blood, urine, vomit, and its cousins ... and hope the risk of infection stayed at bay. We could just hope our amateur caregiving skills were enough to keep her comfortable.

Very unlikely.

We could hope that the moment would not come when the pain was too much because we had no access to medication. We could cross our fingers that she would not fall while we were away as she just became too weak to roll over and throw up into the familiar garbage can.

Very unlikely.

We could hope that she simply passed away peacefully after our amateur caregiving. We could pray that she would not be a party to any of the likely outcomes... bleeding out, hallucinations, fluid fill in the lungs, rampant infection, or something else.

Very unlikely.

And if all our hopes panned out, we would still have to answer to our amateur caregiving. At the end, the police and the coroner would have many questions about an elderly woman dying in her home without any help, starving slowly to death while we looked on and failed to call out for help. We might realistically face criminal penalties for honoring Mother's choices.

Nice.

Choice #2: We could call adult protective services. A caseworker would come to Mother's door. Mother would be very very angry with one or all of us. The caseworker might or might not be able to force caregiving into the home. We might or might not be questioned for our choices. We might or might not emerge from the investigation still intact. We might or might not go to jail.

Choice #3: We could "Baker Act" the situation. Call 911 and EMS would take her to the hospital for a psychological evaluation. We could ask a judge to transfer medical power of attorney to me. I would then have the authority to bring in professional caregivers to a now terrified and traumatized Mother who most certainly would then die, hating me for so brazenly violating her wishes. Any good intentions would become, as is the usual with Mother, irrelevant.

Choice #4: I could walk away from the situation, fly back to Washington, and pretend it wasn't my problem. And, of course, never sleep through the night for the rest of my life.

Four choices, but really no choices.

Despair marched in the door and laughed at both of us, Sol and I. Laughed and Smirked.

Sol and I continued to talk which is exactly what women do when there seems to be no good choice available. Rehash the same issues over and over again, hoping that some other choice would come from the dismal options in front of us.

By the end of the day, after another agonizing round of trying to give care, keeping bedding and Mother dry, and easing the struggle of the ongoing vomiting... our endless discussion landed us in a different place. We plan, we discuss the plan again, and we agree. In the evening, we test the plan.

The fluids on the couch must come to an end. Sol will try to put an adult diaper on Mother. She finagles. She wrestles. No longer asking, Sol gently tells Mother what she is going to do. Sol has overcome a resistance that I thought would never crumble. The diaper is on. The fluids are at bay, for a time. And the test worked. Tell. Don't Ask.

Now, we move on to the greater challenge.

Taking Over

The next morning, we proceeded with the New Plan. Thoughts of Adult Protective Services and the Baker Act thrown to the side, I called the Hospice referral office again, for the umpteenth time in the last few weeks. A wonderful lady there named Sandy had been calling Mother frequently, asking her over and over again if she would like Hospice to help. Sandy continued to call, to try and help despite responses from Mother that ranged from crazy to wholly unpleasant. Sandy was very familiar with the stubbornness at hand. She had worked with German men and women in their last days before. I quickly felt a wave of understanding ripple down the phone line from Sandy's kind heart to my own, shattered heart.

Hospice was only allowed to send an admissions nurse out if Mother consented, but desperate as I was... I asked her to send a nurse out anyway, and Sandy arranged a nurse named Linda to come out in a couple hours time. Mother was not informed. Trouble brewed.

It is easy to think the stubbornness will never yield. It is easy to think that someone will remain the same all the way to the last hours. It is so very easy to buy into an ending without hope.

Hospice

It is all too easy to assume that God walks only through doors to the heart that have been opened wide by free will. That's what they say at church. If the door ain't open, God ain't walkin' through it.

Well, as in most of life, there are some interesting grays in the middle of these dilemmas of free will. Here, God altered his wise old man with the beard visage and transformed into an all loving, all powerful worm. He didn't have a wide open door in Mom's heart to work with. Instead, He had to worm His way in, through tiny cracks in Mom's armor, using His children in perfect ways and good measure. He began today to orchestrate, what do they call that thing, again? Oh, that's right. A Miracle. another one.

Before the nurse Linda came, Sol told Mother that Linda was Sol's friend and also (by coincidence of course), she was a nurse. Sol then simply told Mother that her friend Linda was coming over today to visit Mother. Period. End of discussion.

In that moment, Mother and Sol were the epitome of strong woman pitted against strong woman. I began to wonder if an atomic bomb was about to go off, right here in this small Florida town. Instead, perhaps because so much love was mixed in with that confrontation, Mother said simply "OK."

When the nurse Linda came, Sol and I both looked at each other with that big "Uh Oh! this isn't going to work" exchange. Linda walked in, sat on the couch, connected with Mother, talked to her about Hospice, and repeated what we had told Mother at least one thousand and fifty seven times... No one was going to take her out of her home. Mother could stay at home until she moved on from this world to the next.

Unbelievable that this time, Mother believed. The papers were signed. Help was on the way from the very same Hospice that Mother had derailed, denounced, rejected in every way for months on end, ever since the cancer saga started eight months before.

After the door was closed, Linda on her way, Sol started to cry, with relief. I felt dazed, shocked into silence by what had just passed. Unbelievable. God had crept around all possible corners, through all wee little crevices, and ultimately had His will done in an impossible situation. It wasn't unlike the time in high school, when the impossible scholarship landed on my lap and transformed college from a lost hope to a reality in an instant. Miracles aren't always front page headline type of affairs. Rather, sometimes they were just like this. Impossible outcomes that evolved from impossible circumstances in subtle, crafty, and impossible ways.

Despair ran away for a moment ... intimidated by this turn of events.

Waiting

It would take some time for the Hospice schedule to begin, when a nurse would visit a few times a day. After early evening vigil with Mother, I returned to home base, my head now throbbing with what I thought was a mild headache, nothing more. In just a few hours though, a mild fever had climbed over 100 degrees and the trouble started again.

I went to Mother's side as usual in the late night hours, past midnight, and declined to sleep there, longing for a warm bed to crawl into as my immune system raged some battle against a nameless invader. The little man with the hammer pounded against the inside of my skull, cackling with delight at my pain.

Back in bed, weak and tired at 2 in the morning, I called the 24 hour hospice number, begging for a nurse to come out later in the night so that I could sleep. I was crying, pleading. Tired, lost, and lonely.

Hospice was kind and understanding. The nurse came.

The little man with the hammer shut up, defeated over despair that had once again been averted. As the quiet settled into my head and my body, I slept.

Crisis

By 7 the next morning, Mother was calling and asking for her water. Painfully, I rolled out of bed, fever in tow, and trotted across the street to do her bidding. As I walked through the door, our eyes connected. I saw the familiar anger there. "Whore" she said with her eyes.

I retrieved her water. Waited. Returned it to the refrigerator. I left.

Twenty minutes later, Mary was running across the street, panicked. Mother tried to throw up again into the familiar basket. This time, she fell off the couch and onto the floor. Mary, who had been gone for the four previous days, found her there ... choking and crying out for help.

My fault. As always.

Hospice arrived.

Routine

24 hour care began. Hospice was a constant, reassuring, adept presence in our lives. An abundance of halos now hovered around Mother's house. The hospice nurses came and went, all with unique personalities but all kind, professional, and on the ball. Some are particularly memorable.

Barb bathed Mother from head to toe in a way that profoundly honored her life and her struggle.

Judy had light and laughter in her eyes, even in these dark circumstances. She hugged me when she left, and called me a sweetie. I looked around, and saw only 'Whore'. No sweetie was anywhere to be found.

Evelyn, from South Africa, had the most gentle spirit about her nature. I wished I could bottle it and shower Corporate America with it.

Ruth-Ann who coordinated everyone and everything never once troubled us with an health care insurance issue. She used her quiet strength to ensure that all went smoothly, despite the inevitable Medicare battles going on behind the scenes.

Angel after angel entered the house, chasing away anything dark, whether it resided in the corners of the room or in the center. By Thursday, the house was filled with light. Even Mother's eyes filled with light.

Early Thursday morning, my raging infection now gone thanks to a smashing round of antibiotics, I crept into the house. Mother lay there, weak but bright. Her eyes no longer said "Whore".

Instead, they said "Sweetie".

Hope

God was now clearly of His box. I was no longer limiting what He could do with my own limited view of His power and love. After watching the skillful orchestration of the last few days, where Mother went from a dismal, inadequate caregiving situation to a gold-plated, honoring symphony of many loving and capable caregivers, I had crazy high hope for how the rest of this struggle could now end.

Ecclesiastes tells us that a cord of three or more is far more powerful than one, who is easily broken. And, a cord we were... seeking to bind Mother's heart in peace and love and deliver her to eternal calm and ultimate joy. After watching Mother's anger, pain, and anxiety dominate so much around her for so many decades, now it simply fell away and peace and hope came to fill its place.

God spoke in these final days, using His endearing language through the creatures... ladybugs, butterflies, great blue herons ... all came to the house. Some hovered, some crawled, and some traversed the space with a majestic wing span. Like a movie from Disney, God's creatures came, day after day after day to remind and reassure me of the light that had permanently taken the place of the dark for Mom. I knew she would now go Home when she was done here.

Dying

The Light had its match in the impending death that we were now facing. By evening on the thirteenth day since I landed in Tampa, Mom was hardly speaking at all. Her vocabulary now consisted of barely audible "Water", "Yes", "No" and "Ouch". She was in so very obvious pain whenever she was turned. Some of her pain came from the blossoming bedsore on her backside and some from muscles that lay idle for far too long. Still, she refused all medication and continued to suffer in silence, through the search for sleep, the pain of moving, and through whatever journey she was now traveling in between this world and the next.

Done

Mom had not eaten now in eight weeks; Hospice didn't understand why she was still alive (and neither did we). After falling in love with Mom in the past days, as her heart and personality were transformed by peace that could only come from God, I found it hard to believe that I would now lose her. I couldn't and wouldn't believe it. How could this happen? The sweet loving Mom that I was convinced, for decades, lay under a hard, narcissistic exterior had now popped out, much to my delight. And, now, she would leave.... Really? Whose crazy idea was that?

I was at Mom's side. The fear in her eyes was so sharp that I ached for it to be gone. I looked Mom in the eye and said "Honey... I am so sorry that you hurt ... but you have to let go of the fear and let God deal with it instead. Please, let God do this work for you. Please". Sol followed, with strong loving words "Let go, Let God." And then Ruth-Ann walked in the door and the three of us, with Mom's blessing (a miracle in itself), gathered around her bedside, and prayed. Ruth-Ann led, using all of the right words, the right timing, the right length. Mom relaxed ... she started to slip away.

A few hours later, Mary and my brother-in-law said goodbye.

Sol and I now sat with Mom most of the minutes now. From my ITunes archives, I unearthed some of my Mom's favorite songs from long ago. Then, I played a Christian song whose words I hoped she would hear. The song spoke to the darkness that would now break to light, the shadows that would now disappear.... the faith that would now have to be Mom's eyes.

Mom clearly had one foot here in this world and one foot in the next place, oscillating between the two.

By midnight, when the nurses changed shifts, Mom still had not passed, although the signs from all over, including the Lord, said it was time.

Around 1 in the morning, Sol and I went home to nap. Shortly before 4 a.m., the nurse called. She was halfway through her sentence when I was up and halfway out the door, taking Sol with me. "It's time."

When we arrived, breathing had become even more of a struggle for Mom. She was fully unconscious. I sat down bedside, Sol next to me. I took Mother's hand in mine and I started to sing whatever I could remember. I finally converged onto Amazing Grace and sang the first verse, again and again and again.

Within minutes that seemed like hours, my breath caught as Mom's breath also caught... and held. Then ... there was simply no more breath. Whether the brain decided Enough, or the lungs or the heart, it didn't matter. It was simply over.

The moment hung in the air. Lingering. Just long enough to be permanently etched in memory.

Gone
By the time the White Van came, I was all alone on the front stoop. All had gone cold, even though the sun was still coming up again today. When the White Van rolled into the driveway, I just paced up and down, up and down the sidewalk, singing Amazing Grace.

A few days later, I was back at work. Nothing made sense. People at work were asking for things, many demanding. The responsibilities of home and of work squawked relentlessly at me. I just looked at them like they were crazy.

What do I do now? Could someone please explain to me how to do this?

Epilogue #1

If this were a novel, I would tell you how I grew up, was married, had two children and lived happily ever after.

It just ain't that simple. At 17, I went straight from a small town in Florida to a big city in the Northeast, to a prestigious university where women were rare among the ranks of male engineers. I stumbled, fell, got up, and did it all over again. Without much grace nor the best grades in the world, I graduated at the end of four years, went to graduate school, and then to work. I kept trying.

In the meantime, I went through years of counseling and a trail of failed relationships. I kept trying.

I worked in a male dominated world. I went through years of isolation, marginalization. I kept trying.

I always believed that I would have a child and raise her better than I had been. I would break the cycle. I kept trying.

Instead, Mary became pregnant multiple times followed by multiple abortions. My own body would not carry life.

At forty, I worked as a professor in a male dominated field, neither succeeding nor wholly failing. I taught hundreds of students every year. I loved. I was alone. I kept trying.

A few years later, I married. He loved me. I loved him. I tried. I stumbled. I kept trying. He still loves me. I still love him.

Onward we go.

Epilogue #2

I longed for the mother that Mom would have become if she had continued to live. I would always rejoice that she had gone home to be with God, but I would also at the very same time be deeply sad that our relationship ended, unreconciled. The lack of reconciliation was an ending without an ending. The story that had ended well for Mom had for me, just kept going on, day after day, inconsolable and incomplete.

Over a year later, another crisis came in my life. I turned to those around me, crying for help. Unlike any other time in my life, God sent an army to my side and as the days passed in the latest crisis, one of the angels of the army began to shine brighter and brighter than the rest.

This angel on earth, through the darkness of crisis, would be the light that saved me. Before the crisis, Bonnie was just one of several neighbors. Now, she transformed, almost overnight, into a truly lifesaving gift.

Daily letters from her reminded me that God never leaves, even in the darkest of nights. Bonnie's warm, encouraging spirit, filled with love and strengthened by her own long seemingly pointless struggle ... held me above water, through seemingly endless nights without sleep and long days with no peace.

Of course, it never escaped my notice that this woman, Bonnie, was oh so close to my mother's own age and was also 100% German, just like Mom.

Indeed.

God has His way of reconciling. He doesn't leave Loose Ends.

www.ingramcontent.com/pod-product-compliance
Lightning Source LLC
Chambersburg PA
CBHW051808040426
42446CB00007B/575